Property Taxes, Amenities, and Residential Land Values

Property Taxes, Amenities, and Residential Land Values

A. Thomas King

Ballinger Publishing Company ● Cambridge, Mass.
A Subsidiary of J.B. Lippincott Company

Library of Congress Catalog Card Number: 73-16146

International Standard Book Number: 0-88410-403-6

Printed in the United States of America

Library of Congress Cataloging in Publication Data

King, Alvin Thomas.
        Property taxes, amenities, and residential land values.
        Bibliography: p.
        1. Real property—Valuation—New Haven metropolitan area.
I. Title.
HD268.N38K5   333.3'32'097468   73-16146
ISBN 0-88410-403-6

To My Parents

Contents

List of Figures

List of Tables

Preface

Undoubtedly, most of the interest in this volume centers upon the specific empirical results—the evidence regarding capitalization of property taxes, neighborhood amenities, public services, and accessibility. This is understandable, but in my view there are several aspects of method also worthy of close attention. First, the use of residents' perceptions to describe variations in neighborhood quality is novel and promising. Obviously, questions about the particular treatment can be raised, but in the present case it is clear that perceptions can be obtained in a relatively simple survey, that they describe areas in a very plausible manner, and that they account for a significant proportion of house values. This approach is certainly worthy of more investigation.

Second, I was repeatedly surprised and pleased by the ability of the detailed data available to this study to capture even quite elusive variations. It is not merely that one can account for a large fraction of the variation in market values of single-family homes—more than that, the individual housing components are valued very much as they "should" be. Since the housing market has traditionally been regarded as one of "elusive laws and intrusive variances," these findings seem a strong testimony to the need for high quality, appropriate data bases. The work of collecting original data is arduous and time-consuming, but the question must be asked whether there are not many instances in which the researcher's time is as well spent ensuring that the data used are correct as in devising elaborate econometric techniques to mitigate the deficiencies of standard data resources.

The empirical results of Chapter 5 and much of the discussions in Chapters 2 and 3 appeared in different guise as the first half of my Ph.D. dissertation, "Land Values and the Demand for Housing" (Yale, 1972). Accordingly, my first debt is to the members of my thesis committee: John R. Meyer (Chairman), Peter Mieszkowski, and Guy Orcutt. Professor Meyer was an admirable reader, both quick and attentive. Professor Mieszkowski was extremely generous with his time for discussing procedures and hypotheses. I am almost embarrassed to admit the many hours I must have absorbed.

I am particularly indebted to Professor David Grether, now at the California Institute of Technology, for his patient willingness to discuss solutions to various statistical problems. Professor Neil Singer, my colleague at Maryland, kindly read a late version of the present manuscript and made a number of very helpful comments. To all these persons and the many more who aided in one way or another I am indebted. Naturally, they are not to be held accountable for any errors still remaining.

The manuscript was written and the bulk of the computations completed during the time I have been employed at the Bureau of Business and Economic Research at the University of Maryland. I am grateful to the Bureau and its successive directors, John W. Dorsey and John H. Cumberland, for support, office space, and secretarial assistance. Mrs. Kay Miller prepared an early version of this manuscript and Mrs. Alene Fisher attended to all the late revisions and modifications with competent good humor.

Collection and preparation of the housing data used in this study were supported by a grant from the National Science Foundation to the Institute for Social Sciences at Yale University (NSF–GS3077). The mail survey of homeowners was financed by a separate grant from the Institute for Social Sciences. Initial processing of these data was done with assistance from the Yale University Computer Center; however, most of the work and all of the results reported here were supported by a faculty research grant from the University of Maryland Computer Science Center.

Property Taxes, Amenities, and Residential Land Values

Chapter One

Neighborhood Differences and Location Values

The towns and many small neighborhoods which make up each metropolitan area differ from one another in a variety of ways important to would-be residents. Theoretical models of urban structure generally emphasize differences in the accessibility of various homesites to one or more work places, greater accessibility permitting the residents to save transportation costs and commuting time [3], [25], [28], [50]. Though less often emphasized, the location of the home relative to schools, churches, theaters, museums and shopping districts will also matter. A location near stores selling imported wines and unusual cheeses will have advantages, other things being equal, for households with strong preferences for these items, as shopping trips can be quicker, more convenient and less costly.

However important—or even fundamental—variations in accessibility may be, they are still only a small part of the significant differences among urban neighborhoods. The amenities available in each location matter too: freedom from crime, clean air, low traffic noise, absence of barking dogs, carefully kept neighboring properties, and the like. The local public sector will add its own particular distinctions, since the decision to live in one town rather than another will affect the receipt of public services. Some towns will provide city sewerage and water supply systems, collect garbage quietly and regularly, prune and spray trees, maintain streets and clear them of snow; others will do these not at all or less well. Finally, the statutory property tax burden for identical properties will differ from town to town, depending on the level of services provided and the nature of the tax base.

Do households perceive how neighborhoods differ? If they do, what values do they place on accessibility, amenities, public services, and tax burdens? These questions are the subject of this study.

The basic assumption on which the analysis rests is simple and well-understood: if households perceive neighborhoods to differ, and if greater accessibility, more amenities and services, and lower taxes affect the household's well-being, then any particular household should think it better to live in some neighborhoods than in others.[1] The number of homesites in each neighborhood is necessarily limited, a function of neighborhood size and lot sizes. Competition among households for places in desirable neighborhoods should then result in housing prices being bid up to reflect the advantages of living at that place. We might expect, in other words, the values put on accessibility, amenities, public services, and taxes to be capitalized into location rents.

An interest in rents as a reflection of locational advantage is by no means recent. The role of transportation savings in determining land values is particularly well established, as the principle can be traced back to von Thünen and before him to Ricardo. Recently, numerous empirical studies have verified the existence of location rent gradients in urban areas of the sort accessibility differences would predict [25]. The present study will provide yet another piece of confirming evidence.

Our chief interest, however, will be in determining whether ameni-ties, services, and taxes affect location values. Here the proposition that they should matter is also well established, but the evidence is scanty and unsatis-factory. This is particularly true with respect to property tax differences. That a tax on bare land will be capitalized, causing a reduction in land values, is one of the oldest and probably the most generally accepted statement in the theory of tax incidence. Surprisingly, however, supporting evidence is almost nonexistent. For taxes on reproducible capital there is neither agreement on theoretical expectations nor any very reliable empirical evidence. A study of a prevalent hypothesis—capitalization of the tax into location values—concluded that". . . all the tests of the usually accepted doctrine produced results which are inconsistent with the doctrine" [12, p. 112].

Efforts to relate amenities and services to location rents are more recent than studies of tax capitalization. Air pollution [4, 37, 48], school quality [30], crime [37], parks [46], racial composition [49], and amorphous "amenity" [13] are among the characteristics examined.[2] Despite some success, all of these have relied upon data bases more or less unsatisfactory for the uses made of them. In general, units of observation are too aggregative—census tract data are common—and possess too little detail; what is worse, the deficiencies are often greatest precisely in the measurement of what is most of interest: the neighborhood amenities, property tax burdens, and public services.

As will become clear, the present study is distinguished from previ-ous work not so much in its intention as in what is achieved. In an empirical study of location values the success to be expected is critically dependent on the

1. Of course, there need be no single best neighborhood for all households, as tastes and the places to which accessibility is important can differ.
2. This is not intended to be an exhaustive listing, but only indicative of the aspects considered.

quality and characteristics of the available data base. Good fortune and pains-
taking efforts have compiled a data base for the present study which is uniquely
suited to the demands made of it. It is both disaggregated—being essentially the
sales records for some two thousand single-family homes in the New Haven,
Connecticut metropolitan region—and highly detailed. Among the unusual features are records of the residents' perceptions of neighborhood services and
amenities. The desirability of possessing information concerning perceived
quality in addition to "objective" measures has been noted repeatedly in previous
work, but perceptions have never before been available.

This study is organized as follows: Chapter Two develops the models
of the housing market which are the basis for later empirical work. Chapter
Three describes the data base in detail. As implied above, failure to develop
appropriate measures of neighborhood amenities has been a critical problem in
all previous work. In Chapter Four methods for developing the required measures of *perceived* neighborhood amenities are explained. In addition, characteristics of the property tax system in the United States are examined so that any
special features can be related correctly to the theories of tax capitalizaton. The
empirical work is contained in Chapter Five. Chapter Six compares the present
study with earlier work and attempts to derive some general conclusions.

Chapter Two

Housing and the Housing Market

The theories and assumptions used in the empirical analyses of Chapter Five are discussed here. In the first section, I present the assumptions about the housing market and the housing bundle which are used later to obtain market values for the components of the bundle. Since these assumptions are, to some extent, contrary to conventional wisdom, I examine evidence regarding the more important in section two.

"HOUSING" AS A BUNDLE

"Housing" is one of many commodities which, like "food," are not homogeneous goods, but combinations of many separate and diverse items. Except that they are bought and sold together as parts of a single bundle, these items may have no resemblance and nothing in common. "Housing," for example, consists of such disparate goods as land, water spigots, the right to send children to a local public school, rooms, chandeliers, and insulation. Although these diverse items could, in many cases, be sold separately, this may rarely or never occur. For goods not sold in a market, there is no market price. Yet it is reasonable to suppose that each contributes to the total price of the bundle, and one may wish to know what these contributions are. In the case of "housing," for example, one might wish to know what portion of the total price of a house is due to the presence of a second bathroom. If this contribution can be determined, one may reasonably think of it as the price of the second bathroom, since it is the amount that must be paid to have that feature. Prices of this sort are known technically as "hedonic prices," and in Chapter Five I analyze transaction records for a large number of single-family homes in the New Haven, Connecticut metropolitan region to obtain them for most of the important housing components.[1] Since the property

---

1. For a general discussion of hedonic prices see [1] and [5].

tax burden, neighborhood amenities, accessibility, and public services are all part of the housing bundle, their hedonic prices will reveal the values placed on them.

The Model of the Housing Bundle

It will be convenient to regard the various components of the housing bundle as separable into three general categories: Structural Characteristics (SC), Location Characteristics (LC), and Land (L). Structural Characteristics include such items as the construction material, kinds and quantities of insulation, number of rooms, the house style—whether one-story, two-story, or split level—the kind of plumbing, and the like. The Location Characteristics are all the items which provide utility or disutility to residents at each particular location. They include the various public services available—garbage collection and public schooling—and other more intangible items such as a pleasant view, clean air, friendly neighbors, and well-trimmed lawns. For simplicity, the property tax obligation for the dwelling unit is also included here. Land is simply land. The housing bundle is then defined as the sum of these:

$$\text{Housing Bundle} = \sum_{i=1}^{m} SC_i + \sum_{j=1}^{n} LC_j + L. \tag{2-1}$$

The sales price of the bundle is taken as the sum of the price per unit of the Structural Characteristics, Location Characteristics, and Land, multiplied by the quantities of each in the bundle:

$$\text{Sales Price} = \sum_{i=1}^{m} \alpha_i SC_i + \sum_{j=1}^{n} \beta_j LC_j + \gamma L. \tag{2-2}$$

Estimates of the prices of the housing bundle components, the α's, β's, and γ, will be obtained in Chapter Five by regressing the sales price of the bundle on the physical measures of the components. This procedure requires a strong assumption which should be stated clearly: the contribution of each component to the total price of the bundle is assumed to be constant throughout the sample and therefore independent of the overall composition of the bundle or its physical location. In other words, two-car garages are assumed to add equally to the value of both a suburban mansion and an urban hovel, provided that the garages themselves are identical.[2]

2. It is desirable to emphasize that the analysis assumes only that *identical* components will have identical prices. It seems likely that an immediate denial of this important assumption may be based on comparisons of unlike items. Thus the urban hovel's garage may be quite different from that of the mansion's, though they are both two-car garages. Proper quality controls for the components can make the assumption of uniformity more palatable.

Uniform pricing within the metropolitan housing market is an assumption which many persons will find objectionable. Commonly, pricing is believed to be chaotic or irrational and, therefore, to exhibit little or no regularity and certainly not the degree which I have assumed.

> The absence of a market place, the private and secret nature of transactions, the want of comprehensive market data, all combine to deprive the housing market of the benefits of a visible price structure. Both buyers and sellers, in varying degree, operate in the dark. . . . The ultimate uniqueness of every house makes it impossible to establish uniform sales units or standards of value. [44, p. 209]

Despite its entrenched position, the folklore of irrational pricing is in conflict with the conclusions of recent empirical studies. They find that the housing market is not one in which the prices of identical items vary drastically, but one in which pricing patterns do show considerable regularity and uniformity.

> The picture that emerges . . . is that of an orderly marketing process for real estate. . . . The "goodness of fit" belies the common assertion that housing markets are chaotic, irrational, monopolistic and therefore not amenable to empirical generalization.[3]

While the charge of complete irrationality and chaos is easily rejected, there is a plausible, more moderate possibility for consideraton. It might be suggested that uniform prices are probable within small areas—submarkets of the metropolitan area—but the assumption is not appropriate to a large region. In this view, the prices for housing bundle components should be determined by supply and demand functions, like the prices of any other market commodity. The relevant question then becomes: over what geographic area is it reasonable to assume constant demand and supply relationships?

On the supply side, it is clear that the housing built in each period will reflect that period's technologies, tastes, and relative factor prices. If a city is built checkerboard fashion, each square in a different time, the area of similar supply functions could be quite small. On the demand side, buyers may consider themselves restricted to what is available in only a small area for a number of reasons: reluctance to move from an ethnic neighborhood, racial discrimination, desire to be close to work and old friends, a wish to live within a particular school zone.

Potentially, then, supply will be unadjustable and stylized by date of construction; and demand, fragmented. The consequence could be great variation in housing prices between submarkets of the metropolitan area, though prices within the submarket would be regular.

3. William C. Pendleton, "Statistical Inference in Appraisal and Assessment Procedures," *Appraisal Journal,* 33, No. 1 (January 1965), pp. 73–82.

The possibility just described can certainly not be rejected out-of-hand, yet there are reasons to doubt that price variations between submarkets will, in fact, be very great in the New Haven region studied. Most important, the entire region is small, making it possible to live almost anywhere and be within thirty minutes of a work place. Considerations of accessibility, then, should not lead to greatly fragmented demands. Second, the variety of supply within even small areas, like census tracts, is quite large.[4] Within New Haven proper—and to a lesser extent elsewhere—particular areas were developed all at once and bear the marks of the period. But, in most places, new construction remains a possibility, thus supplies are less stereotyped and uniform than might be expected. Besides introducing variety, new construction tends to promote uniform prices by preventing the creation of positive quasi-rents. With new construction, a potential buyer can have whatever features he wants at the cost of replacement, which is relatively uniform throughout the region.

In sum, while the market may indeed be segmented, the variations in prices of identical components are probably reasonably constrained. Though it would be possible to modify the assumption of uniform prices throughout the entire metropolitan area and identify separate submarkets for housing, this would greatly complicate the analysis; I shall therefore retain the assumption of strict uniformity on the ground that the error involved is small and quite tolerable for the investigation here.[5]

The Prices

The analysis of the housing bundle will yield estimated prices for three kinds of components: Structural Characteristics, Location Characteristics, and Land. Hedonic prices for the Structural Characteristics are often of great interest and usefulness, particularly for the construction of cost-of-living indexes [27]. But, except for some minor use as benchmarks to evaluate the reasonableness of the estimates in this study, they have no importance here. Prices for the remaining two kinds of components are, in contrast, of very great interest.

The price paid for the land component of the housing bundle is expected to reflect the access to centers of economic activity. In general, the greater the accessibility, the lower the transportation costs which a resident at that place will incur, and the savings should be capitalized into the price of the land. The expected pattern of variation in land prices can be shown rigorously with the help of a simple model.[6] Assume that the metropolitan area contains a

4. This is examined in more detail subsequently.

5. Elsewhere [18], I have examined price variations within the region and find them, in fact, to be fairly moderate. This is true in particular for those components of greatest interest here: neighborhood amenities, accessibility, and taxes. It seems likely that the market for these components is areawide since the choice of amenities is presumably an important part of the choice of location.

6. The model presented here is a slightly more disaggregated version of that in Muth [28]. A number of other persons have developed similar models, for example, [3] and [50].

single, centrally located employment center, the Central Business District (CBD), to and from which households make a fixed number of trips each day. Transportation costs for the household consist of money outlays on vehicle operation or transit fares and the time costs of travel. The former are roughly proportional to the distance traveled, but the latter are a function of the distance traveled, the rate of speed, and the value placed on time spent in travel.

For simplicity, I will assume the commuter values time spent in travel in terms of the income foregone by traveling rather than working; he may, however, value time spent commuting at only some fraction of his wage rate.[7] The particular assumption made here about the valuation of time is, in any case, not important for this study because of a second simplifying assumption I make, that the transportation network is equally good in all directions from the CBD.[8] In this case, direct money outlays and time costs of travel both increase with distance from the CBD and have a fixed relationship to one another for travel in all directions. Consequently, there is no need—or possibility—to distinguish time costs from cash outlays, and the distance traveled will serve as an acceptable proxy for both.

The household is assumed to be able to purchase housing bundles combined as it wishes from the m Structural Characteristics, the n Location Characteristics (neighborhood amenities), and Land. Prices of all characteristics but Land are assumed constant, and Land is sold at a price which depends on the distance to the CBD. It is easy to show that these assumptions imply the existence of a land rent gradient, having a peak at the CBD and falling uniformly with distance.

Assume that the household has an ordinal utility function

$$U = U(Z, H, A, L),\qquad\qquad (2\text{-}3)$$

where

Z = dollars worth of all other goods including the value of leisure

H = vector of m possible components of the housing bundle

A = vector of n location amenities, assumed to be a function of the location θ of the bundle, $A = A(\theta)$

L = amount of land.

7. The proposition that persons value leisure or commuting hours by the income foregone in not working is deeply rooted in economic analysis. It is, for example, fundamental to the usual analyses of the effect of income taxes on the labor–leisure choice. For commuting hours in particular, there is, however, very little evidence that the wage rate of the traveler correctly values his time. Becker [6, p. 510] suggests that about 40% of hourly earnings may be about the right value. Other persons have suggested that commuters may actually value trips of moderate length as welcome interludes between work and home [23, p. 50].

8. This assumption will be examined elsewhere in this chapter.

The budget constraint for the household is assumed to be[9]

$$Y = Z + p_H H + p_A A + p_L(D)L + T(Y,D),\qquad(2\text{-}4)$$

where

Y = income per period

p_H = vector of m prices of housing components

p_A = vector of n prices of amenities

$p_L(D)$ = the price per unit of land, assumed to be a function of the distance D from the CBD

$T(Y,D)$ = the cost of transportation, where

$$\frac{\partial T}{\partial Y} > 0, \frac{\partial T}{\partial D} > 0.$$

The utility function, the budget constraint, and the amenity function may be combined using the method of Langrangian multipliers to yield:

$$V = U(Z,H,A,L) + \lambda[Y - Z - p_H H - p_A A - p_L(D)L - T(Y,D)] + \mu[A - A(\theta)].$$
$$(2\text{-}5)$$

The first order conditions for this function to have a maximum[10] with respect to the decision variables, Z, H, θ, L, D, are

$$\frac{\partial V}{\partial Z} = \frac{\partial U}{\partial Z} - \lambda = 0 \qquad(2\text{-}6)$$

$$\frac{\partial V}{\partial H} = \frac{\partial U}{\partial H} - \lambda p_H = 0 \qquad(2\text{-}7)$$

$$\frac{\partial V}{\partial \theta} = \frac{\partial U}{\partial A}\frac{\partial A}{\partial \theta} - \lambda p_A \frac{\partial A}{\partial \theta} = 0 \qquad(2\text{-}8)$$

$$\frac{\partial V}{\partial L} = \frac{\partial U}{\partial L} - \lambda p_L(D) = 0 \qquad(2\text{-}9)$$

9. It should be apparent that p_H, p_A, and p_L in equation (2–4) are the prices paid per unit of H, A, and L consumed per time period. Thus, these prices differ from the α's, β's, and γ of equation (2–2). A trivial conversion is necessary to convert the former prices into the latter.

10. I assume that the necessary second order conditions are fulfilled.

$$\frac{\partial V}{\partial D} = \lambda \left(\frac{- \partial P_L L}{\partial D} - \frac{\partial T}{\partial D} \right) = 0 \qquad (2\text{-}10)$$

Differentiating with respect to λ and μ yields, respectively, the budget constraint and the amenity function.

Equations (2-6) to (2-9) yield the usual conditions for utility maximization; namely, that the ratio of marginal utilities be equal to the price ratio for each pair of commodities. However, equation (2-10) is of greatest interest at this point, as it can be rearranged to yield

$$-L\frac{\partial P_L}{\partial D} = \frac{\partial T}{\partial D} . \qquad (2\text{-}11)$$

This states that when the household is in equilibrium the change in expenditures on land which results from a small change in distance must equal the change in transportation costs which results from the move.[11] Since, by assumption, $\partial T/\partial D$ is greater than zero, $\partial p_L/\partial D$ must be less than zero, or land prices must fall with distance.

This simple model has an important implication for empirical analysis of the land rent gradient which, though it is quite obvious, has not always been recognized.[12] From equation (2-4) it is apparent that the amount spent on land in each housing bundle will depend both on the distance the land is from the employment center and on the quantity of land purchased. Some previous studies have proceeded, however, to analyze the change in the value of the housing bundle with distance as if this were independent of the amount of land purchased. For any given purchaser, the transportation saving which results from a move closer to the center of employment is independent of lot size, but it should have been recognized that this does not permit the purchaser to pay only a lump sum for the privilege of moving an identical housing bundle closer to work. The purchase of a housing bundle involves a choice both of location with associated transportation costs and of a quantity of land in this location. The lower the transportation costs, the higher the price of land per square foot and so the smaller the amount of land purchased.

Location Characteristics

The Location Characteristics differ from the Structural Characteristics and Land because the household cannot purchase them directly, but must instead act indirectly by purchasing a location having the desired attributes. For example, in putting together a housing bundle, no one can purchase a scenic view or pleasant neighbors as such; instead one must purchase a location pro-

11. See [28], pp. 23-9.
12. See [35].

viding access to these desirable things. More generally, the location of the house's physical structure within a town, census tract, and school district provides the purchaser with the opportunity and sometimes the unavoidable obligation to consume a varied package of public services and natural amenities. Location determines the taxes to be paid on a house of a given assessed value, the quality of the public schools which children can attend, the amount of damage and discomfort which air pollution will cause, and the danger from criminal activities. For obvious reasons, the Location Characteristics are often known as neighborhood effects or locational amenities.

It can be expected that the amenities available at each location will influence the total sales price of the housing bundle. Differences in amenities and taxes, just like differences in accessibility, will affect the utility that a household receives from residence in a particular place. As they seek to increase their utility and compete for locations with high amenity levels and low taxes, households should bid up the price paid for each location to reflect the value to them of the different services. The result will be formation of "bumps" and "hollows" on the otherwise smoothly declining accessibility land rent gradient.

This study will examine the effects of several specific kinds of neighborhood amenities. First, the property tax burden is considered for evidence of capitalization. As shown subsequently, the opportunity for capitalization is ample because the effective property tax rates vary by fifty percent within the metropolitan area. Second, the value placed on various public services is obtained; these include municipal garbage collection, water supply and sewage disposal systems. I distinguish these particular programs because some towns do and others do not supply them at public expense; moreover, private supply is always possible using private collectors, wells, and septic tanks. Since each service is essential and the cost of private supply clearly known, the possibility of capitalization into location value seems quite great.

Third, the influence of less specific amenities is considered. These include public services provided in all towns where the difference between locations is mostly quality of service. These are such things as street maintenance, education, police and fire protection. The treatment of these amenities is a primary distinguishing feature of this study: for the first time, it has been possible to construct measures of *perceived* location amenities in addition to various "objective" measures. The sources of these data and the construction of the indexes are fully described in Chapters Three and Four.

AN EXAMINATION OF ASSUMPTIONS

In the previous section, several important assumptions were made about the economic structure of the metropolitan area, the transportation network, and the variety of housing bundles available to purchasers within small areas. These were convenient and facilitated exposition, but they require examination and some modification before being used in an empirical analysis.

The Land Rent Gradient

The model used to demonstrate the changes in land prices within a metropolitan area assumed that all economic activity occurred in the CBD. The need to travel to the CBD for work or shopping meant that transportation costs for the household rose as it moved away from the CBD, and land prices were shown to fall with distance from the CBD as a consequence.

The severe monocentric assumption of this model is not, however, an accurate description of even single cities, and certainly not of the entire New Haven metropolitan area consisting of more than ten separate towns. Greater realism can be achieved by generalizing the monocentric assumption to recognize that the metopolitan area has numerous centers of economic activity to which access has value. By the arguments above, households that work in the various centers of economic activity will compete for locations close to their workplaces and will bid up the land prices to reflect the savings they realize in transportation costs. Thus, each place of employment will be the center of a rent gradient, and the land rent surface for the metropolitan region will not decrease smoothly and uniformly in all directions as the distance from the CBD increases. Instead, the height of the land rent surface at each point will depend on the potential savings due to accessibility from that point to all places of economic activity and on the competition for land at this location.

Thus, if I assume, as above, that the access from each location to a place of work is a function of the distance between them, a suitable measure of the total accessibility of the location would be

$$\text{Access} = \sum_{i=1}^{m} f(D_i) \tag{2-12}$$

for $i = 1, \ldots, m$ work places. This measure of the accessibility of each location is deficient in one important respect: no allowance is made for the possibility that the location is highly accessible only to minor employment centers. At such locations, it may be possible for all those households wishing to be near their place of work to be accommodated without causing an increase in the price of land that would reflect their transportation savings. In other words, the majority of bids for these locations may come from persons working at large, distant centers for whom transportation savings are small. Local workers must overbid only these low offers to obtain their desired location.

These considerations suggest modifying (2-12) to be

$$\text{Access} = \sum_{i=1}^{m} \alpha_i f(D_i) \tag{2-13}$$

where α_i is the importance of the ith center. The measure of accessibility given in equation (2-13) is sometimes known as the gravity concept of human inter-action, since the importance or "pull" of each center may be regarded as proportional to its size and as inversely proportional to the distance, or distance squared, between the employment center and the residential location.

A measure of accessibility such as equation (2-13) appears to be a reasonable generalization of the simple monocentric model to recognize the spread of economic activities throughout the metropolitan region. For empirical work, however, this measure has the defect of being tedious to calculate when many places of employment are distinguished. Fortunately, a complete measure of access is often unnecessary; examination of equation (2-13) indicates that whenever non-CBD employment is widely and evenly distributed, the variations in accessibility measured at various points in the region will depend entirely on the changes in the distance from those points to the CBD. Employment opportunities in non-CBD centers, in these circumstances, are offsetting and can therefore be ignored in the computation of accessibility [28, pp. 215].

The data available for the examination of the actual pattern of economic activity in the New Haven metropolitan region are given in Table 2-1, as figures showing the number of work trips ending in each tract of the New Haven SMSA. Despite some inaccuracies and omissions, these data, derived from the work trip origin-destination matrix of the 1967 New Haven Special Census, are the best available for examining the distribution of jobs.[13]

Table 2-1 indicates that the CBD (defined here as census tracts 1, 2, 3, 17) is not the only destination of work trips, which invalidates the simple monocentric model. However, it is the destination of 21,331 work trips, which is more than 25% of the total work trips reported and is a far more important employment center than any other place. Outside the CBD, only tracts 18 and 38 receive more than 4,000 trip-ends, and none of the rest receives more than 2,400. The only place of concentrated employment opportunities outside the CBD is the extreme northwest corner of tract 38, where one industrial area accounts for 3,071 of the 4,091 jobs in that tract.

The entries in Table 2-1 imply that the assumption of a dominating CBD with widely scattered local employment is not unreasonable. Figure 2-1 shows this graphically. It can be seen that although the variation in the number of trip-ends among tracts outside the CBD is substantial, most tracts are within a

13. The only areas included in the present study which are completely omitted from this table are Cheshire and Wallingford. The Census was of the New Haven SMSA and so did not include these towns. Coverage of the SMSA itself is to some extent incomplete because of difficulties encountered by the Census in tabulating incomplete or vague responses.

A brief description of this Census, not including the tabulations presented in Table 2-1, can be found in U.S. Bureau of the Census, *Current Population Reports,* Series P-28, No. 1459, "Special Census of the New Haven SMSA, April 5, 1967," (Washington, D.C.: Government Printing Office, 1967).

Table 2-1. Distribution of Journeys to Work by Census Tract

Census Tract	Number of Work Trips with this Destination	Census Tract	Number of Work Trips with this Destination
1	12204	19	1350
38	4091	27	1225
18	4039	55	1135
3	3817	13	1134
17	2781	54	1035
2	2529	43	1007
44	2361	15	1003
22	2213	25	901
7	2116	6	894
8	2111	12	827
20	2013	52	721
41.02	1901	35.02	697
56	1885	51	661
40	1786	14	658
16	1757	9	634
24	1712	26	603
23	1524	45	551
31.01	1509	48	537
39	1445	46	504
50.04	1443	5	473
21	396	36	184
37	378	57	175
60	371	41.01	167
32.01	351	58	146
30.01	345	50.03	137
62.01	332	11	128
4	326	32.02	126
35.01	308	42	119
47	287	31.02	115
10	265	34.02	99
49.01	247	34.01	67
29	227	33	57
61	222	50.02	54
59	219	30.02	22
50.01	207	62.02	10
28	185	53	5

Source: Special tabulation of the origin–destination work trip matrix from the 1967 Special Census of the New Haven SMSA.

short distance of one or more of the important secondary employment centers. Thus, the locational advantage of being close to a secondary center is an advantage fairly evenly shared. It must be remembered too that the entire SMSA is relatively small and travel times between points are not long.

    The wide and fairly even distribution of non–CBD employment in the New Haven SMSA suggests that calculation of the complete measure of accessibility is probably not worthwhile. Although for different cities, the

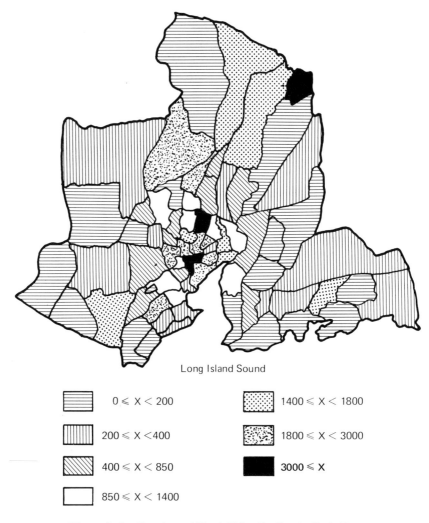

Long Island Sound

$0 \leqslant X < 200$	$1400 \leqslant X < 1800$
$200 \leqslant X < 400$	$1800 \leqslant X < 3000$
$400 \leqslant X < 850$	$3000 \leqslant X$
$850 \leqslant X < 1400$	

Figure 2-1.   Number of Work Trips Ending in Each Tract

findings of several previous studies support this position. In his detailed study of the value of accessibility in the Washington, D.C. area, Pendleton [35, pp. 22-5] found high simple correlations of various measures of employment potential and distance from the CBD. Muth [28, p. 215] similarly reports simple correlations of -0.89 to -0.98 between measures of manufacturing and retail employment potential and distance from the CBD of South Chicago. For these reasons, I shall examine the variation in land values in the New Haven metropolitan region with respect primarily to the distance from the property to the CBD. In appearance, this procedure is indistinguishable from using the simple monocentric assumption, but the rationale is different and more acceptable.

For comparision with this, a simplified version of the general employment potential measure (2-13) is also tested to see if there might be some advantage to the more complex measure. The simple version will recognize only two employment centers, the CBD and the industrialized portion of tract 38. Recognition of these two centers would seem to be a reasonable approximation to the more complete measure of employment potential.

Travel Times from the CBD

The discussion above of the land rent gradient relied upon an important simplifying assumption; namely, that the network of roads permitted equally rapid travel in all directions from the CBD. The importance of this assumption lies in the simplification it permits in the empirical estimation of the land rent gradient in Chapter Five. Although transportation costs are assumed to consist of two distinct parts—time costs and vehicle operation costs—the assumption of equally rapid travel in all directions means that both components of total costs will increase in the same proportion for distance traveled in any direction. Thus, the land rent surface will slope downward smoothly and equally in all directions from the CBD. If, however, movement from the CBD is quicker in some directions than in others, then the time costs of travel will increase more slowly in some directions than in others, and the slope of the rent surface will vary with the direction of movement from the CBD.

In addition to smoothing and making uniform the rent surface in the metropolitan region, the assumption of equally rapid travel in all directions has another consequence of importance for the later empirical analysis. If it is tenable, then distance traveled will be an acceptable proxy variable for both time and vehicle operation costs of travel, and no attempt is necessary to distinguish between their separate effects. Distance being easier to measure than costs, this is a worthwhile advantage.

The reason one might suspect the validity of this important and very convenient assumption is that segments of two interstate freeways pass through portions of the New Haven metropolitan region, as shown in Figure 2-2. It seems possible that work trips using these freeways will be quicker than those of equal length which pass over city streets.

Table 2-2 contains the information needed to evaluate the assumption of equally rapid travel in all directions. The table shows the time required for the journey using the fastest routes.[14] and the speed of travel. The entries in

14. The travel times were taken from the 1968 Skimtree matrix supplied by the Connecticut Department of Transportation, Division of Transportation Planning. The travel times are averages of peak and off–peak measurements, adjusted by the Department to reproduce actual traffic flows in a computer simulation of the road system. The Department's courtesy and assistance in providing and explaining these data are gratefully acknowledged.

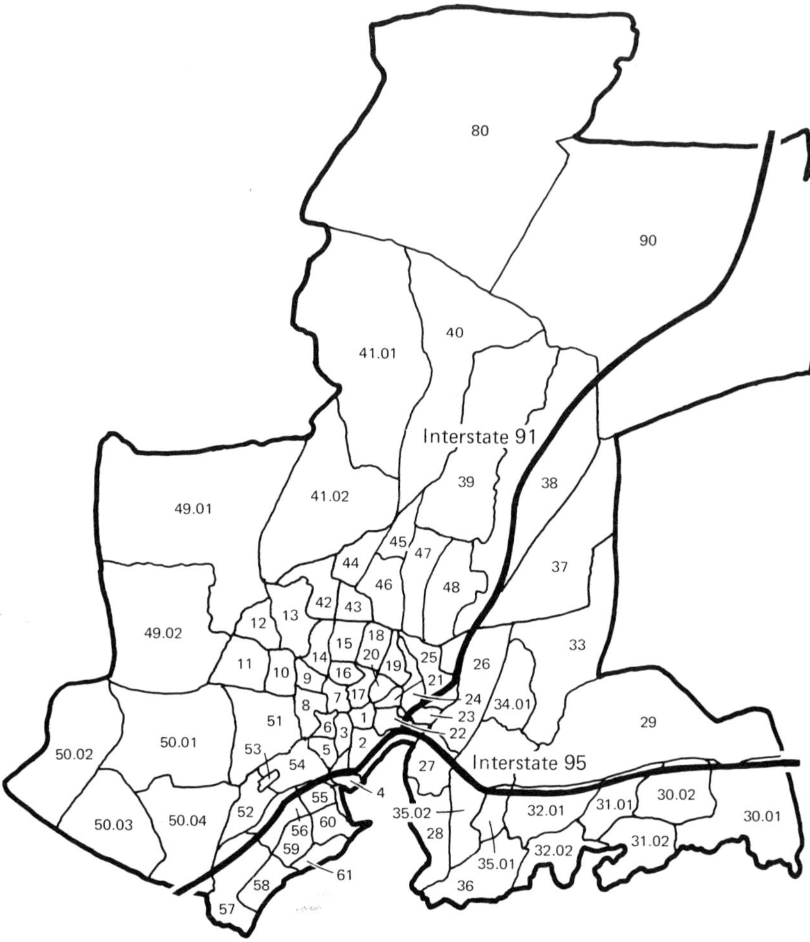

Figure 2-2. Location of Interstate Highways in New Haven Metropolitan Region[a]

[a]Census tracts shown for each town.

the table are striking in several respects. One is the rather short distances from tract 1 to other tracts, which result in short travel times. The entries suggest that most work trips in this region are probably less than fifteen minutes long. A second point of interest is the wide variation in the travel speeds between tracts, from a low of 1.7 mph to a high of 33.7 mph. By excluding the very short trips for which errors in measuring times or distances will cause the calculated speeds to vary wildly, one can reduce the range of fluctuation considerably. Even so, in

Table 2-2.   Distances, Travel Times, and Speeds from Census Tract 1 to Other Tracts within the New Haven Metropolitan Region

Tract	Distance (Miles)	Time (Min.)	M.P.H.
1	–	–	–
2	.67	3	13.4
3	.10	3.5	1.7
4	1.24	3	24.8
5	1.05	4	15.8
6	.71	4	10.7
7	.67	5	8.0
8	1.19	7	10.2
9	1.52	8	11.4
10	2.14	9	14.3
11	3.10	13	14.3
12	3.29	13	15.2
13	2.76	11	15.1
14	1.86	8	14.0
15	1.71	8	12.8
16	1.00	7	8.6
17	.57	3.1	11.0
18	1.52	5	18.2
19	1.43	5	17.2
20	.71	3	14.2
21	.76	4	11.4
22	.57	2	17.1
23	1.43	4	21.5
24	1.43	6	14.3
25	1.90	7	16.3
26	2.71	8.3	19.6
27	1.86	6.6	16.9
28	3.14	12	15.7
29	6.19	15.6	23.8
30.01	9.05	18.5	29.4
30.02	7.33	16	27.5
31.01	6.00	13	27.7
31.02	6.90	16.5	25.1
32.01	4.57	12	22.9
32.02	5.48	17	19.3
33	5.38	12.6	25.6
34.01	3.52	10	21.1
34.02	3.14	14[a]	13.5[a]
35.01	3.62	10	21.7
35.02	3.29	8	24.7
36	4.57	16.5	16.6
37	4.86	11	26.5
37[b]	7.00	16	26.3
38	4.76	12	23.8
38[b]	5.71	13	26.9
38[b]	7.86	14	33.7
39	5.33	14	22.8
39[b]	7.86	16	29.5
40	6.57	17	23.1
40[b]	9.29	22	25.3
41.01	7.14	17	25.2
41.01[b]	9.14	21	26.1

Table 2-2 (continued)

Tract	Distance (Miles)	Time (Min.)	M.P.H.
41.02	5.00	17.5	17.1
42	3.10	15	12.4
43	2.38	11	13.0
44	3.52	14	15.1
45	4.14	12	20.7
46	2.76	10	16.6
47	3.10	11.5	16.2
48	3.33	12	16.7
49.01	5.71	18	19.0
49.02	5.00	19	15.8
50.01	4.52	15.2	17.8
50.02	6.86	21.5	19.1
50.03	6.29	17	22.2
50.04	4.86	12.5	23.3
51	2.38	9.7	14.7
52	3.43	11	18.7
53	2.67	—	—
54	1.81	8	13.6
55	2.00	7	17.1
56	2.95	10.5	16.9
57	4.76	15	19.0
58	4.38	13.5	19.5
59	3.24	11	17.7
60	2.48	9	16.5
61	3.05	11	16.6
80	12.52	27.2	27.6
90	11.00	20.2	32.7

[a]The time and hence the speed calculated for this tract would seem to be incorrect. Probably they should be much the same as for tract 35.02.

[b]These tracts have been subdivided into inner and outer portions because of their sizes and shapes.

Source: Connecticut Department of Transportation supplied the travel times. The distances were measured on a map of the region. See note 14 infra.

an initial examination too much variation seems to remain to make the hypothesis of equal speeds plausible.

The appearance of substantial variation is, however, somewhat misleading, as much of the remaining variation results from general increases in traffic speeds in all directions as the distance from the CBD increases. For example, the travel speeds from tract 1 to 17, 18, 46, 45 and 40 increase regularly with distance, from 11.0 mph to 25.3 mph. Presumably, this results from decreasing congestion on the roads. Variation from this source does not, of course, reflect in any way on the validity of the hypothesis being considered.

Evaluation of the hypothesis requires comparing the speeds of travel to tracts equally far from the CBD. When this is done, the speeds for journeys which can use the freeways is sometimes quite close to speeds for journeys which cannot. For example, a nonfreeway trip of 9.14 miles to tract 41.01 has a speed of 26.1 mph, whereas a freeway trip of 9.05 miles to tract 30.01 has a speed of 29.4 mph. A similar comparison for tracts 45 and 32.01 yields speeds of 20.7 and 22.9. Therefore, the times required to make journeys of similar lengths are in some cases very much the same, even when the roads used would seem to be of differing quality.

Counter-examples to those cited can, of course, be readily found. For example, the nonfreeway trip of 5.71 miles to tract 49.01 is at a speed of 19.0 mph as compared to the trip by freeway of 6.0 miles to tract 31.01 at a speed of 27.7 mph. Careful examination of Table 2-2 seems to support the conclusion that journeys from tract 1 which use I-91 or I-95 (to the east) are indeed somewhat faster than trips of equal length which do not use freeways, provided that the tract of destination is very near the freeway. The advantage of the freeway appears to vanish quickly if more than a little travel on local roads is required after leaving the freeway, as it is, for example, to reach tract 36. Probably this is because the total distance traveled is so short that the absolute advantage of high-speed freeways is limited. This rationale is consistent with the observation that the opportunity of using I-95 for the short trips westward to tracts 52, 54, 55, 56, and 57 permits average speeds no greater than for most trips within New Haven.

The advantage in speeds offered by freeways to some tracts in the metropolitan region is not trivial: a trip to tract 31.01 is about 30% faster than one to tract 49.01. Nevertheless, the importance of the advantage is not clear: because the journeys are fairly short, the absolute advantage in minutes saved is not great, and one might suspect that a commuter will not be very sensitive to a small saving of time. Moreover, the advantage of the freeways is limited to those tracts immediately adjacent to them; for most of the other tracts the speeds are nearly equal in all directions. These considerations suggest that the assumption of equal speeds in all directions is probably tolerably accurate. I shall, therefore, use it in the empirical analysis, but will scrutinize the findings in Chapter Five for evidence of error from doing so.

Small Area Variation of Housing Bundles

The decision to treat the entire New Haven metropolitan area as a single housing market depended on the conclusions that demand would not be too geographically fragmented nor supply inflexible. The small size and quick internal access of the area demonstrated above tend to support a conclusion of relatively uniform demand. In this section, I examine the housing bundles available within single census tracts to determine how limited is the choice within a small area. The more uniform the housing stock, the more likely it is that a rare bundle will have significant quasi-rents.

Table 2-3. Combinations of Housing Bundle Components[a]

Tract (1)	House Size vs Quality (2)	House Size vs Lot Size (3)	Number of Observations (4)
4	2	1	3
5	7	2	15
6	5	2	6
7	2	1	2
8	3	3	3
9	5	3	10
10	7	4	25
11	5	4	23
12	6	4	34
13	3	3	9
14	5	4	36
15	6	3	19
16	1	1	1
18	6	5	15
19	6	3	11
20	4	3	4
23	1	2	2
24	1	1	1
25	4	2	4
26	8	7	34
27	4	3	11
28	7	6	42
29	6	6	16
30.01	4	3	5
30.02	3	4	14
31.01	2	1	2
31.02	2	2	2
32.01	4	4	5
32.02	5	4	7
33	6	8	71
34.01	7	5	19
34.02	2	5	8
35.01	5	5	14
35.02	6	4	29
36	6	5	35
37	8	8	27
38	9	7	89
39	8	8	104
40	9	9	78
41.01	5	6	39
41.02	7	7	44
42	7	7	27
43	6	3	26
44	6	5	44
45	5	3	42
46	9	8	42
47	6	7	39
48	4	5	32
49.01	9	7	53
49.02	7	5	35
50.01	5	5	43

Table 2-3   (continued)

Tract (1)	House Size vs Quality (2)	House Size vs Lot Size (3)	Number of Observations (4)
50.02	5	4	22
50.03	7	5	46
50.04	4	3	15
51	7	6	37
52	6	7	20
54	5	4	12
55	3	2	16
56	6	5	21
57	7	4	31
58	8	7	41
59	3	3	18
60	6	4	15
61	4	3	9
80	9	9	176
90	8	10	113

[a]For an explanation of this table see note 15 of the text.

Table 2-3 indicates that even within census tracts the combinations of house size and quality and house size and lot size are quite varied.[15] Tabulations not presented indicate that the variation in the number of rooms of houses within each census tract is also substantial. Therefore, a household should be able to find houses in each location that combine lot sizes, house sizes, number of rooms, and overall quality in numerous ways, and one of these should be very nearly what it wants. Table 2-4 shows the simple correlations for some of the components included in the present study. These generally moderate correlations suggest that efforts to establish market prices for components will not be stymied by problems of multicollinearity.

15. This table indicates the variety of combinations of house size, quality, and lot size available within each area to prospective buyers. Houses in each tract were divided into three classes by their floor size in thousands of square feet: (0.0-1.0), (1.0-2.0), (2.0- and over). Four classes of overall quality were distinguished: Excellent, Very Good, Good, Fair or Poor. Lots were divided into four classes by tens of thousands of square feet: (0.0-1.0), (1.0-2.0), (2.0-4.0), (4.0- and over).

Housing bundles were then cross-classified by house size and quality and house size and lot size within each tract. The numbers in columns (2) and (3) are the number of cells which had entries for that tract. Column (4) indicates the total number of sales in the tract.

As an example of how to interpret this table, consider the entries for tract 28. The table indicates that the 42 observations included housing bundles with 6 of the 12 combinations of house size and quality and 6 of the 12 combinations of house size and lot size. The combinations most often missing include those with the lowest quality.

Table 2–4. Correlations Among Housing Bundle Components

Component	Correlations											
SIZLOT[a]	1.00											
FACBSS	0.07	1.00										
SQFT	0.29	0.27	1.00									
ROOM/S	-0.17	-0.14	-0.59	1.00								
HARDWD	0.15	0.22	0.60	-0.37	1.00							
EXCLNT	0.16	0.20	0.48	-0.27	0.40	1.00						
BASMNT	-0.02	-0.00	0.09	-0.10	0.22	0.04	1.00					
BATHS	0.29	0.23	0.60	-0.23	0.41	0.34	-0.01	1.00				
VOLTS	0.07	0.10	-0.01	-0.00	0.08	0.14	-0.02	0.06	1.00			
ZONES	0.14	0.10	0.20	-0.00	0.16	0.17	-0.08	0.24	0.05	1.00		
GAR 1	-0.19	-0.09	-0.23	0.14	-0.11	-0.09	0.03	-0.25	-0.03	-0.09	1.00	
SALE	0.00	0.06	0.08	-0.00	0.03	0.04	0.00	0.08	0.01	0.00	-0.04	1.00

[a]See Table 5–1 for definitions of the variables.

Chapter Three

The Data and Their Preparation

The empirical results of this study, to be presented in Chapter Five, are based on the analysis of two distinct but complementary bodies of data collected especially for this study. The first of these is a set of detailed descriptions of the physical characteristics of many single-family homes; the second, a set of descriptions of the neighborhoods in which these homes are located. This chapter describes these data and their preparation for use in the empirical analyses.

CHARACTERISTICS OF THE HOUSING UNITS

Data Source

The sample of dwelling units consists of 1892 single-family homes located in the towns of New Haven, Hamden, North Haven, East Haven, Woodbridge, West Haven, Orange, Cheshire, Wallingford, and Branford, Connecticut. Observations, therefore, are drawn from all but the three outlying and largely rural towns of the New Haven SMSA.[1] In addition, observations from Cheshire and Wallingford have been included in this study, following the practice of the regional planning agencies, though the towns are not actually in the SMSA as defined by the Bureau of the Census. Figure 3-1 is a small map of this area.

With a few exceptions, these 1892 observations include all the single-family homes sold in these towns through the Multiple Listing Service (MLS) of the Greater New Haven Board of Realtors in the period January, 1967 to September, 1969.[2] As a source of information about houses and housing transactions, the files of the MLS are unique and extremely valuable. Briefly, the MLS operates as follows: real estate brokers who are members of the service

1. North Branford, Guilford, and Bethany are excluded.
2. The cooperation and assistance of the Board of Realtors in making these data available for this and other studies are gratefully acknowledged.

Figure 3-1. The New Haven Metropolitan Region

agree that a description of any house listed for sale with them will be sent to the central MLS office if they are unable to sell it themselves in a short time. When the MLS office is notified of a house offered for sale, it prepares a description of the features of the house in a standard format and distributes this to all member brokers. In this way, knowledge of the sales offerings in the housing market is widely disseminated, to the advantage of the sellers, the potential buyers, and the member brokers. The description of the physical features of the house, the seller's asking price, the sales price, and date of sale are kept on file in the MLS office. These records provide a wealth of detail about the houses passing through the housing market, and of the workings of the market itself. Almost all of the information about the individual houses included in this study was obtained directly from the MLS files and transferred to punch cards for use. The only exception is the number of square feet of living area in the house, which was usually obtained from the records of the town assessors.

Data Characteristics

For these data, as for any other, it is important to consider the possible inaccuracies and biases. Evidence that houses sold through the MLS are unrepresentative of all houses sold in the region or that MLS transaction records are inaccurate would obviously impair the generality and usefulness of the conclusions which can be drawn.

Fortunately, the question of accuracy can be evaluated with considerable confidence. The descriptions and sales prices of the homes were collected by the realtors for their own use in selling the house and in collecting the fees; thus, it is reasonable to accept them as highly accurate. If more than minor, random inaccuracies existed, the descriptions would inconvenience and embarrass brokers using the service. If the problem were severe, the MLS would be useless. Without belaboring this point, it is important to emphasize the high accuracy of these housing data because much subsequent analysis depends upon this.[3]

In contrast to the question of accuracy, the possibility that houses sold through the MLS are a nonrandom selection of all houses sold cannot be dismissed out-of-hand, as the MLS sales account for well under half of all houses sold.[4] Yet there are no very persuasive reasons why this fraction should be greatly unrepresentative of the larger market. It does seem likely that houses which are hard to sell because of their location, absolute price, or special features will be a larger proportion of MLS sales than of non–MLS sales. These houses will require the wide market which multiple listing provides, whereas the common, average house can be sold by the owner or the original broker. Therefore, one might expect very high–priced, and perhaps also very low–priced, houses to make up a mildly disproportionate share of the MLS sample. One type of sale which is likely to be underrepresented in the MLS sample is that involving houses whose sales prices are not representative of general market conditions. For example, houses sold at a nominal price to relatives will not pass through MLS. As I have noted, the MLS acts to widen the housing market and improve the

3. One aspect of the question of accuracy is not so happily resolved. Because of the incompleteness of some descriptions, a problem of missing data is created. The treatment, described in the third section of this chapter, will introduce occasional minor inaccuracies. But this does not alter the larger conclusion that descriptions actually given are correct.

4. Conversation with Mr. Paul Gates of the Greater New Haven Board of Realtors.

shopper's knowledge of offerings and relative prices. This implies that sales prices relative to features may be more uniform than they are in the non–MLS market. For the present study, these considerations would seem to be no reason to avoid using MLS data, as they simply eliminate transactions and spurious variations which are unrepresentative of the general market.

A satisfactory empirical test of how representative MLS sales are of the total market is, unfortunately, not possible because no statistics for non–MLS transactions are available. This is true for simple comparisons such as the location of houses sold and the distribution of sales prices; and, of course, it is also true for more detailed comparisons. There is, for example, no possibility of learning whether MLS transactions involve, on the average, houses with larger or smaller lots, more or fewer bathrooms, appliances, or fireplaces than do non–MLS transactions.

The only tests of representativeness which can be made on the basis of existing statistics involve comparing the MLS transaction flow with the housing stock reported in the 1967 Special Census of the New Haven metropolitan area.[5] For many reasons, such comparisons are unsatisfactory; yet, because they are the only comparisons possible, I present several in Tables 3-1 and 3-2. No formal statistical tests for differences will be made because of the unsatisfactory nature of the comparisons involved.

From Table 3-1, it appears that the MLS sample has relatively more high–priced houses than does the Census count. This may reflect, in part, the greater tendency of high–priced homes to pass through the MLS, as I have hypothesized. However, some of the difference might also result from the substantial increase in housing prices during the period 1967-69. This would be reflected in the MLS price distribution, but not in the Census figures which were collected early in 1967.

Table 3-2 indicates that MLS homes are scattered widely and fairly evenly among the Census tracts, the count of MLS homes being about 3 to 5% of the Census count in most tracts. A few tracts, mainly those having few single-family homes, have no or few MLS sales. The worth of these comparisons, however, depends on whether the turnover rates in all tracts are similar, and no information on these is available. The comparisons of house values in Table 3-2 show that the means of the MLS sales tend to exceed the means of the Census count values by about 10%, which is as expected given the inflation over the period. In summary, though it would be incorrect to place much weight on the evidence of Tables 3-1 and 3-2 because of the unavoidable use of inappropriate data, probably the MLS sample includes relatively too many of the high–priced homes. But how serious a problem this is, is unclear, since it is likely that com-

5. A brief discussion of the Special Census is contained in U.S. Bureau of the Census, *Current Population Reports,* Series P-28, No. 1459, "Special Census of the New Haven SMSA, April 5, 1967."

Table 3-1. Distribution of Values of Single-Family
Owner-Occupied Homes

Price ($000)	Percent of Total[a]	
	Census	*MLS*
0.0– 5.0	0.4	0.0
5.0– 7.5	0.8	0.6
7.5–10.0	1.6	1.4
10.0–12.5	4.2	1.5
12.5–15.0	8.5	4.2
15.0–20.0	32.0	24.0
20.0–25.0	22.0	26.0
25.0–30.0	12.0	16.0
30.0–35.0	7.5	9.0
35.0–	11.0	18.0

[a]Numbers may not add to 100 because of rounding.
Source: Special Tabulation of the 1967 Special Census of the New Haven SMSA.

parisons of MLS sales with non-MLS sales would show greater similarity than do these comparisons of MLS sales and housing stocks.

CHARACTERISTICS OF THE NEIGHBORHOODS

Data Sources

Information available to this study about the neighborhoods within the New Haven region is of two kinds: first, "objective" descriptions of various characteristics including pupil–teacher ratios and the amount of air pollution. Such data have been used in previous studies and the particular series available here were not especially unusual; they are described in more detail in Chapter 4. The second kind of neighborhood data are "subjective" or perceived descriptions. The availability of these is one of the significant distinguishing features of this study, and to evaluate their usefulness it is quite important to understand their source.

The data series of perceived neighborhood characteristics was obtained using a mail survey of the purchasers of the homes in the MLS sample. Sent in early February, 1970,—or about six months after the last MLS sale had occurred—the survey form requested that the homeowners evaluate thirteen neighborhood characteristics such as public elementary school quality, danger of crime, and bus service.[6] The questionnaire set a two week deadline for the return of the booklet; and immediately before this was reached, a post card

6. In addition, considerable other information about the household was collected, but these data are not directly relevant to the present study. A reproduction of the portion of the survey described here is found in Table 4-9.

Table 3-2.   Comparison of Mean Values and Number of Homes by Census Tracts

Census Tract	Census Mean Value ($000)	MLS Mean Value ($000)	MLS Value as Proportion of Census Value	Number of Houses from Census Count	Number of MLS Sales	MLS Sales as Percent of Census Count
1	15.39	—	—	7	—	—
2	14.62	—	—	6	—	—
3	16.11	—	—	79	—	—
4	14.81	12.53	0.78	117	3	2.6
5	13.93	12.15	0.87	183	16	8.7
6	14.13	10.20	0.72	120	8	6.7
7	21.79	25.15	1.15	53	2	3.8
8	16.87	19.17	1.14	125	3	2.4
9	25.35	26.09	1.03	172	10	5.8
10	28.59	30.68	1.07	771	25	3.2
11	32.12	30.42	0.95	713	23	3.2
12	19.23	19.92	1.04	694	34	4.9
13	22.84	26.04	1.14	161	9	5.3
14	28.13	30.32	1.08	588	37	6.3
15	16.12	14.78	1.13	496	20	4.0
16	12.11	13.80	1.14	160	1	0.6
17	34.56	—	—	17	—	—
18	37.12	40.87	1.10	258	15	5.8
19	25.94	36.14	1.39	313	11	3.5
20	29.77	33.26	1.12	116	5	4.3
21	16.52	—	—	15	—	—
22	19.48	—	—	11	—	—
23	15.48	14.20	0.92	77	3	3.9
24	13.75	22.50	1.64	111	1	0.9
25	15.70	12.55	0.80	271	4	1.5
26	17.26	19.91	1.15	1093	34	3.1
27	18.14	17.30	0.95	525	12	2.3
28	21.06	21.39	1.02	1186	42	3.5
29	23.81	28.69	1.20	566	16	2.8
30.01	26.33	39.50	1.50	433	5	1.2
30.02	28.99	36.47	1.26	578	14	2.4
31.01	19.18	17.50	0.91	594	2	0.3
31.02	23.14	33.33	1.44	687	3	0.4
32.01	18.68	17.52	0.94	272	5	1.8

32.02	20.27	19.03	0.94	601	7	1.2
33	18.23	19.39	1.06	1501	69	4.6
34.01	17.71	18.16	1.03	464	19	4.1
34.02	18.70	19.54	1.04	403	8	2.0
35.01	18.81	19.87	1.06	509	14	2.8
35.02	18.41	19.42	1.05	1212	30	2.5
36	16.87	16.84	1.00	1133	36	3.2
37	24.08	29.80	1.24	1224	27	2.2
38	21.59	23.54	1.09	2091	90	4.3
39	30.87	34.10	1.10	1948	104	5.3
40	23.68	26.53	1.12	1744	79	4.5
41.01	26.62	30.24	1.14	878	40	4.6
41.02	25.18	27.10	1.08	1373	44	3.2
42	19.38	21.61	1.12	1100	27	2.5
43	17.86	18.03	1.01	636	26	4.1
44	19.53	21.17	1.08	1261	44	3.5
45	22.31	24.88	1.12	699	42	6.0
46	23.93	24.19	1.01	951	43	4.5
47	34.33	39.14	1.14	804	41	5.1
48	21.96	25.87	1.18	999	32	3.2
49.01	35.24	41.04	1.16	886	54	6.1
49.02	37.94	40.69	1.07	728	35	4.8
50.01	32.54	36.88	1.13	1203	43	3.6
50.02	34.32	38.54	1.12	574	22	3.8
50.03	34.83	37.17	1.07	943	46	4.9
50.04	31.42	36.25	1.15	509	15	2.9
51	18.17	18.40	1.01	1032	37	3.6
52	19.84	22.89	1.15	645	20	3.1
53	6.30	—	—	1	—	
54	16.74	18.75	1.12	491	12	2.4
55	17.38	17.04	0.98	471	16	3.4
56	19.87	21.87	1.10	586	22	3.8
57	18.35	20.16	1.10	1447	31	2.1
58	17.95	19.99	1.11	1705	41	2.4
59	19.51	18.81	0.96	592	20	3.4
60	16.74	18.09	1.08	928	15	1.6
61	16.34	14.90	0.91	330	10	3.0

Source: Special tabulation of 1967 Special Census of New Haven SMSA. Census counts are for owner-occupied single-family homes.

reminder was mailed to those who had not yet responded. After two more weeks, a second questionnaire and a more urgent cover letter were sent to the remaining nonrespondents. No further efforts were made to obtain responses.

Questionnaire forms were sent to approximately 1900 homes in the New Haven metropolitan area, and of these, slightly more than 45% were returned with fully usable information. The detailed description of the response is given in the following table.

Table 3-3. Response to the Mail Survey

Number	Percent	
1919		Total mailed out
– 11		Vacant houses
– 15		Returned—no such address
1893	100.00	
1043		Survey forms returned
– 57		Blank
986	52.09	Overall response
– 13		Renters
– 3		Ministers (house bought by church and rented)
970	51.24	
–107		Omitted because of missing data, possible wrong respondent, other causes
863	45.59	Total usable responses

The exact questions on the mail survey form and the preparation of the responses for use in this study are described in Chapter Four. What is important here are the characteristics of the responses. Accurately reported evaluations are, of course, essential, and it is important that they come from a representative sample of the MLS purchasers. If only a small and highly selective portion of those surveyed returned their forms, little weight can be attached to their evaluations. I consider first the problem of accuracy.

Accuracy: Several studies indicate that although biases in the returns of mail surveys are common, the accuracy of the answers themselves may not be a serious problem. In his excellent general discussion of questionnaire design and survey methods, Oppenheim [32, p. 33] does not suggest that inaccuracy is characteristic of data obtained from mail surveys. Indeed, he cites a study which compared the results of a mail survey and personal interviews which requested information about the occupational grade of the respondent. In this study, an 88% agreement between the two methods was obtained.[7]

McDonagh and Rosenblum [21] report a study in which they sent questionnaires to a group of persons and then interviewed a sample of both the respondents and the nonrespondents. They found no significant differences in the responses either between the mail answers and the interview answers of respondents or between the interview answers of respondents and nonrespondents. They concluded that for their study entirely satisfactory information could have been obtained from their mail survey alone, although their response rate was only 46.1%

A third study, by Daniel C. Rogers [38], investigated the accuracy with which incomes were reported in mail surveys, examining with particular care the accuracy of recall for incomes over the preceding fifteen years. Rogers chose a sample of nonfaculty employees who had been employed at Yale University from 1950 to 1965, and gave them a short questionnaire concerning their total annual earnings and hourly rates in each of the years 1950, 1955, 1960, and 1965. As a check on the responses, he was able to use the W-2 records of taxable earnings from the personnel office. The null hypothesis he tested was that the annual earnings from the records were equal to the annual earnings reported in the questionnaire. This hypothesis could not be rejected at the 5% level for any of the four years investigated. His finding that reported and recalled incomes could be accepted as accurate is valuable and quite relevant to the present study, since the respondents were requested to report what their incomes had been in each of three years, 1967, 1968, and 1969.

The studies of accuracy just described cannot, of course, establish that the data in the present study are also accurate, but they may help dispel suspicions. Unfortunately, only somewhat limited direct tests of the accuracy were possible. Ideally, one would evaluate what is reported in the questionnaire by comparing it to data from a second, independent source known to be correct. Personal interviews to gather a second set of responses were infeasible, and without them the possibility for this kind of direct test was limited to comparisons using the questionnaires and the MLS data. Obviously the MLS could have no information regarding the purchaser's subjective neighborhood evaluations, so there is no possibility of testing this. What is done instead is to examine several other responses for accuracy.

Each respondent was asked the date on which the house was purchased, something known from the MLS cards. Frequently, there was disagreement; however, this was not surprising. What the MLS reported was the deposit date, the time the house was removed from the market by an accepted contract.

---

7. There is no obvious reason to resolve this discrepancy on the assumption that the interview yielded the correct answers.

The date of legal transfer and possession might occur as much as eight or ten months later, and is the date the respondent would most likely report. This test of accuracy is, therefore, weak; at most, it can be said that a discrepancy of three months or more was uncommon.

A related series of checks were made whenever the deposit date and the reported purchase date differed by more than three months. According to assessment records and deeds, a number of the large differences resulted when the respondent accurately reported a sale subsequent to the MLS transaction.

If the difference between purchase dates could not be resolved as an indication of a later sale, an additional check was made. The city directory for the appropriate address was consulted, and the occupation reported there for the resident at the address was compared to the occupation reported by the respondent. If these were not the same, it was assumed that the survey form had been filled out by the wrong household and the response was omitted from this study. The number of responses which were deleted in this process was rather small, which indicates that, for those questionnaires examined, the occupations and places of work were usually reported accurately.

By far the most important direct test of accuracy was a comparison of actual and reported prices for former homes. Among the questions on the form sent each household was one asking for the address and sales price of the former home. About 180 households reported owning a single-family home in the New Haven metropolitan area previously; search of the transaction records from the Board of Realtors found that 38 of those families had used a realtor to sell this home. Thus, from the two sets of data there were available exactly the kind of information required for a really satisfactory examination of response accuracy: the actual sales price from the realty records and the reported sales price from the questionnaire form.

The results of the comparison, summarized in Table 3-4, are quite encouraging. Of the 38 responses, 19 were exactly correct; another 13 differed from the correct amount by $500 or less, a minor difference which is probably due to the questionnaire asking "*about* what did this home sell for?" The remaining six larger discrepancies are shown in Table 3-4.

Thirty-eight responses obviously constitute only a small fraction of the total sample, and for that reason it is necessary to weigh this evidence with some caution. Nevertheless, there is no basis to suppose that the households for whom this check could be made were more likely to be honest or accurate than those for whom it could not. In this regard it is worthwhile to note that respondents to the questionnaire could not have known that their replies were subject to the kind of cross-examination described, for no mention was made of the realty records, and the cover letter implied that the sample population had been randomly selected from among all homeowners in the area. On the whole, the evidence of this comparison is an implication of accuracy in the responses to questions on mail surveys.

Table 3-4. Comparison of Reported and Actual Sales Prices on Former Homes

Reported Price ($000)	Actual Price	Error
31.5	29.9	1.6
12.9	15.9	3.0
34.0	31.0	3.0
18.0	16.0	2.0
21.0	20.0	1.0
43.0	45.0	2.0

Number of Exactly Correct Responses: 19
Number of Responses Correct within $500: 13

In addition to these direct tests, two indirect tests provide evidence which, though less convincing by itself, tends to support the conclusion that inaccuracy is not a major problem. The first of these tests is extremely simple. From previous studies, it is known that housing purchases and family income are closely related. Thus, one way to gauge the accuracy of income reporting is to correlate income with housing values. The data showed a simple correlation of greater than +0.65 between these two measures, which, with almost 900 degrees of freedom, is highly significant. The relationship is, in fact, stronger than that found in most previous studies, a result anticipated from care taken in the design of the study. This outcome provides some additional evidence of reasonably accurate responses.

A second piece of indirect evidence is obtained from studying the distribution of reported incomes.[8] Many studies have found the Pareto Law of Income Distribution to fit the observed distribution quite well for that segment above the income mode [11, p. 54]. This law may be stated as:

$$N(y) = Ay^{-\alpha} \qquad (3-1)$$

where $N(y)$ is the number of incomes above y. By taking logarithms of both sides, the equation is converted for a form in which the parameters are easily estimated by least squares regression.

Using census data and other reasonably accurate official sources, previous studies have estimated α to be 1.9 to 2.1, with some indication that it is increasing over time [11, p. 57]. When the parameters of (3-1) were estimated for the present data set, α was found to have a value of 2.2. This implies that the

8. The evidence from examination of income distributions is, of course, dependent on the condition that households in the sample reporting incomes above the mode be properly representative of all households with similar incomes. The representativeness of the sample is discussed subsequently.

income distribution for respondents *in the upper income portion of the sample* is very similar to distributions from samples for which the question of accuracy is less urgent. This suggests, in turn, that respondents have exhibited either remarkably consistent biases and offsetting inaccuracies or have, in fact, been tolerably truthful in their reported incomes. Naturally, evidence of this sort cannot settle the question of inaccuracy in responses, but it does cause one to doubt that great inaccuracies exist.

Response Bias: The problem of bias in data derived from mail surveys is well known;[9] Oppenheim [32, p. 33], for example, in a discussion of the relative merits of various survey techniques, has commented that "a mail questionnaire cannot hope to cover people of low intelligence or of very limited educational background." As a written document, the questionnaire form is certain to be answered more easily and more often by persons who comfortably read and write. This implies that the mail survey is not an appropriate means of gathering information from a representative sample of the general population, as the responses will tend to reflect disproportionately the opinions of the intelligent, well-educated, and relatively wealthy. A second source of bias in the responses is that of respondent self-selection. Persons interested in or informed about the questions being asked are more likely to respond than are the disinterested and uninformed.

These sources of bias suggest that the responses to the present survey cannot be accepted without critical examination. Nevertheless, one may anticipate that bias of the usual sorts is likely to prove less troublesome to this study than to many others. This is because the population sampled is not representative of the general population; as the owners of single-family homes, they have, on the average, higher incomes and more education than would a random sample of the total population.[10] Therefore, the persons most likely not to respond to a mail survey have been excluded at the outset. One cannot expect this to eliminate the problem of relative oversampling of the well-educated and higher income groups, but the problem should be lessened.

Similarly, one cannot expect that all households on the mailing list will have been equally interested in a housing study; nevertheless, since they all are recent movers, they must necessarily have been involved in the housing market and have probably made some evaluation of the kind of neighborhood they have chosen to live in. Their relative levels of interest and information about housing are likely, therefore, to be more comparable than would be those of a general cross-section of the population. Moreover, a special effort was made to encourage a favorable attitude toward the study. Just before the questionnaires

9. Christopher Scott [40] presents a careful review of the literature on mail surveys.

10. For some evidence of this see Martin David, *Family Composition and Consumption* (Amsterdam: North Holland Publishing Co., 1962), p. 56.

Table 3-5.   The Comparative Distributions of Families by Total Money Incomes

	Percent of Total	
Incomes ($000)	*Census*	*MLS*
0.– 4.	11.2	1.3
4.– 5.	4.4	0.9
5.– 7.	11.1	3.8
7.– 9.	15.7	10.0
9.–15.	37.1	47.0
15.–15.	16.7	26.6
25.–	3.7	10.0

Source of Census data: U.S. Bureau of the Census, *Current Population Reports,* Series P–60, No. 75, "Income in 1969 of Families and Persons in the United States" (Washington, D.C.: U.S. Government Printing Office), Table 16: Type of Residence and Race–Familes and Unrelated Individuals by Total Money Income in 1969. The figures given here are for white families in metropolitan areas under 1,000,000 population.

Table 3-6.   Educational Attainment Levels of Persons 25 Years of Age or Above

Years of School Completed	*Census*	*MLS*
0– 8	22.1	6.4
9–11	16.4	8.6
12	36.4	28.0
13–15	11.8	17.0
16	8.1	17.0
16–	5.2	23.0

Source of Census data: U.S. Bureau of the Census, *Current Population Reports,* Series P–20, No. 207, "Educational Attainment: March, 1970" (Washington, D.C.: U.S. Government Printing Office), Table 2: Years of School Completed by Persons 25 Years Old and Over, by Type of Residence, Age, Race, and Sex for the United States: March, 1970. The figures given here are for white residents of both sexes of metropolitan areas. The figures for the MLS survey are for all persons over 25 in 1967.

were mailed, a short discussion of metropolitan housing problems was inserted in the leading local newspaper, *The New Haven Register.* The article described some of the housing–related problems which interest economists and added that a study of the New Haven area would begin soon and would include a survey of many homeowners.

With these preliminary remarks in mind, what specifically can be said of the representativeness of the respondents? It is easily seen from Tables 3-5 and 3-6 that the distributions of respondents by family income and by the education level completed by persons twenty–five or older are unlike those of the general population. But this difference only confirms what was expected and tells one nothing about the relevant question of whether homeowners who responded to the survey differ systematically from those who did not.

Ideally, what is required is information about both respondents and nonrespondents regarding such things as income, education, and age, since these are the items expected to be associated with strong biases. This is rarely available following mail surveys, and the present study is no exception. There is, however, some unusually good indirect evidence which can be used to evaluate response bias.

The first, and more conventional, test for bias follows from the suggestion that late respondents resemble nonrespondents [32, p. 34]. Thus, if it appears that distributions of early and late respondents by income, education, age of head, family size, etc. are similar, one might suspect that nonrespondents are not markedly different from respondents. The second test to be made is unusual and valuable because it closely approximates the ideal test we would like to make to compare actual income distributions. Specifically, from the realty records, we have the purchase price for each of the homes sold. These are known with little or no error and in no way depend upon information supplied by the respondents. As noted previously, many studies have found very close relationships between the household's income and some other socio-economic characteristics and the value of housing purchased. Thus, if it appears that the distribution of respondents by value of house purchased is unbiased, it is likely that the distribution by income and other characteristics is also unbiased.

Comparison of Early and Late Respondents: The comparison tests of early and late respondents were made in the following manner: fifty-one responses were chosen at random from among those received in the first ten days of the survey, and an additional fifty-one were chosen from those received in late March, when the flow of responses had decreased to only a few each day. The respondents in each group were compared on the basis of four characteristics: age of the head of the household, education of the head, the household's 1969 before-tax income, and the number of persons in the family. For each of these a Chi-square test was made of the hypothesis that the distribution of values observed in the late returns could have resulted from a random sample drawn from a population having the distributional characteristics of the early returns. The test values and degrees of freedom for each hypothesis tested are given in Table 3-7.

If the rejection level for the hypotheses tested is set at 0.05, the calculations of Table 3-7 permit the rejection of only one hypothesis, that of similarity of family sizes in early and late respondents. From an inspection of the distributions, it appears that the late respondents tend to have either large or small families. Although the hypothesis of similarity of educational levels is not rejected, comparison of the distributions indicates that late returns have a reduced proportion of heads with more than a college education. Similarly, the

Table 3-7. Comparisons of Early and Late Respondents

	Received before 22 February	*Received after 21 March*
Age of Head		
20–29	16	12
30–34	11	9
35–39	6	6
40–44	6	10
45–49	7	6
50–	5	8

$$\chi^2 = 5.99 \text{ d.f.} = 5 \qquad P \approx 0.30$$
$$\chi^2_{0.05} = 11.1$$

Education of Head		
0– 8	4	3
9–11	4	5
12	12	20
13–15	4	6
16	7	5
16–	20	12

$$\chi^2 = 10.61 \text{ d.f.} = 5 \qquad 0.05 < P < 0.10$$
$$\chi^2_{0.05} = 11.1$$

1969 Income		
0– 8999	6	9
9000–10999	7	10
11000–12999	9	9
13000–14999	7	7
15000–18999	7	6
19000–24999	7	3
25000–	8	7

$$\chi^2 = 5.33 \text{ d.f.} = 6 \qquad P > 0.50$$
$$\chi^2_{0.05} = 12.6$$

Family Size		
1–2	9	12
3	17	6
4	14	15
5	5	6
6–	6	12

$$\chi^2 = 14.40 \text{ d.f.} = 4 \qquad P < 0.01$$
$$\chi^2_{0.05} = 9.49$$

very low χ^2 value calculated for income distributions provides no evidence that the late respondents and presumably the nonrespondents differ from the early respondents; nevertheless, closer examination of the income distributions suggests the need for caution. Note that the number of persons reporting incomes under $11,000 has increased somewhat among the late respondents, and the number with incomes over $15,000 has decreased.

It is evident that these tests of bias yield mixed results. On the one hand, a formal test does not permit one to reject the hypothesis of similarity; but, on the other hand, the changes in the overall distributions are toward a greater concentration of low income and education households in the later returns. Extrapolating the apparent tendencies would suggest that nonrespondents would be less well educated and have lower family incomes than would respondents. The extent of these biases is probably not very great, however.

Distributions of House Values: To obtain a better indication of the magnitude of response bias in the survey, we turn to the second test available, a comparison of the distributions of sales prices for the homes of respondents with that of the total sample. The hypothesis to be tested is that the distribution of sales prices of respondents' homes can be regarded as a random sample drawn from the total population of MLS home sales prices. The data for this test are presented in Table 3–8.

The value of χ^2 is sufficiently small that the hypothesis cannot be rejected at the 5% level, yet there is a question whether it is proper to conclude from this formal test that bias by socio–economic class is absent. The response rates of households in high value homes is markedly higher than that of households in low value homes, and the simple χ^2 test takes no consideration of the nonrandom character of these differences.

The evidence we have obtained in all these tests regarding the magnitude of the response bias by socioeconomic class is easily summarized but not

Table 3–8. Comparison of the Prices of Homes for the MLS Sample
and the Respondent Subsample

Values ($000)	MLS Sample	Respondent Subsample[a]	% Response Rate
0 –10	31	7	23
10 –12.5	24	6	25
12.5–15.0	72	24	33
15.0–20.0	453	185	41
20.0–25.0	530	251	47
25.0–30.0	307	150	49
30.0–35.0	169	82	49
35.0–	331	158	48

$\chi^2 = 12.2$

$d.f. = 7$

$\chi^2_{(0.05)} = 14.1$

[a]Respondents were taken to be only those who returned a usable questionnaire. The outcome of the test is not much altered if the respondents were defined to include those returning partially incomplete forms.

unequivocal. The formal χ^2 tests of bias have not been enough to reject the hypothesis of similarity of respondents and nonrespondents. Nevertheless, there was a consistent tendency for later respondents to have somewhat less education and lower incomes than early respondents. Similarly, the rate of response for purchasers of high value homes was markedly greater than that for purchasers of low value homes, but the difference was not significant statistically. Overall, the suggestion of bias in the direction expected in mail surveys seems more plausible than a lack of bias, but this is less obvious than is usually held.

The important implications of these tests for our use of the data are these: while some bias probably exists because respondents are unlikely to be a perfectly representative sample of housing purchasers, the bias is probably quite slight. This is shown by the general failure to reject the hypotheses of random selection. Even more important, for our purposes, a correction for any slight bias is probably unnecessary. Table 3-8 revealed that purchasers of high-priced homes were about twice as likely as purchasers of low-priced homes to respond. But the sample surveyed[11] consisted very largely of the former. Excluding purchasers of homes selling for less than $15,000—only about 7% of the population surveyed—the response rate varied only from 41% to 49%. Thus, any system of weighting would make only slight differences.

THE TREATMENT OF THE DATA

In preparing these bodies of data for use, it was necessary to make various assumptions which will be explained here. The main problem encountered in the description of housing characteristics was one of missing data. The MLS cards provided richly detailed descriptions about each house, but these were not always exhaustive of all possible items. For example, a description of one house might note that the house had a slate roof as a special feature. If one were concerned about the type of roofing as an influence on value, one would wish to include the feature "slate roof" in the hedonic price regressions. However, for many houses no information was provided about the type of roofing, so that it was not possible to describe the house definitely as either having or lacking the slate roof; thus, a problem of missing data arose. With few exceptions, this problem was resolved by assuming that, if the house was not stated to have the feature, then the house did not have it. This seemed reasonable, since the purpose of the cards was to supply information about the special features of the house which might appeal to the buyer. This assumption was applied to missing data for insulation, hardwood floors, basements, sewer and water connections, laundry rooms, garages, fireplaces, and the like.

Missing data for a few other features were treated differently. When the construction date of the house was missing, it was filled in as the mean of the

11. Not merely the respondents.

construction date for the other houses sold in that same census tract. If the date of sale was missing, it was assumed to have occurred ninety days after the house was put on the market. Every house was assumed to have at least one bathroom. The few houses for which assessments at the time of sale were not given and could not be obtained subsequently from the assessor's records were omitted from the study. Finally, for a few houses, information about the heating system was missing, and these also were omitted.

Chapter Four

Property Taxes, Services, and Amenities

This chapter examines the property tax system, local public services, and locational amenities to prepare for the empirical work which follows. In the case of property taxes, the main task is to develop the hypothesis of tax capitalization; for public services and amenities the problem is one of measurement.

THE PROPERTY TAX

An Overview

Understanding the economic impact of the property tax is important both because the tax itself is important and because for this tax there is unusually clear evidence of apparent inequities, vertical and horizontal. Viewed as a part of the total revenue system, the tax may not seem particularly significant. Alone, it raises only somewhat more than 10% of all receipts for federal, state, and local governments, but in the United States by tradition and statute only the local governments actually rely to any extent on the tax. For these governments the property tax provides nearly 90% of all tax revenues. Consequently, any effort to assess the fiscal impact of local governments must consider the problem of property tax collections (Table 4-1).

In addition to the rather large absolute collection of about forty-four billion dollars in 1972, the other prominent characteristic from a national point of view is the variation in tax rates from under 1% to well over 4% of market value. This variation can be welcomed as evidence of healthy diversity in tastes and the ability of the local public sector to respond, particularly when high taxes are joined with fine services. Or it can be condemned as inequitable, particularly in the many instances where wealthy communities enjoy low taxes and fine services while nearby poor regions endure high rates and poor services. For the purpose at hand, however, what is important is merely to emphasize the

Table 4-1. Property Tax Collections

| | Amounts ($million) | | | Percent of Total Tax Revenue | | |
Area	Total	State	Local Government	State & Local	State	Local
United States	24,670.1	834.0	23,836.1	43.5	2.8	87.1
Northeast	7,218.0	17.5	7,200.3	45.1	0.2	82.8
North Central	7,615.0	287.1	7,328.6	48.6	3.7	92.8
South	4,398.8	194.9	4,204.4	33.0	2.3	84.0
West	5,438.1	334.8	5,103.1	46.3	5.6	88.6

Source: U.S. Bureau of the Census, *Census of Governments, 1967.* Volume 2, Table 1.

Table 4–2. Median Effective Tax Rates of Cities by Region

Median Effective Tax Rate (percent)	*Number of Cities*				
	Total	*NE*	*NC*	*South*	*West*
Total	122	25	34	39	24
4.0 or more	2	2	–	–	–
3.5–3.99	2	2	–	–	–
3.0–3.49	9	6	2	1	–
2.5–2.99	13	8	5	–	–
2.0–2.49	27	3	8	7	9
1.5–1.99	39	2	16	11	10
1.0–1.49	21	2	3	12	4
under 1.0	9	–	–	8	1

Source: U.S. Bureau of the Census, *Census of Governments, 1967.* Volume 2, page 15.

great variation in tax rates and note that these may have little or no relation to public service differences (Table 4–2).[1]

For the individual taxpayer, what is important is both the amount of tax to be paid and the equity of the liability; it is on the latter account that the property tax has traditionally been criticized most severely. Any individual's property tax liability is supposedly a function of the market value of property owned and the tax rate imposed by the jurisdiction. The charge of horizontal inequity derives from the general impossibility of determining the market value of most property accurately. Since no more than a minor fraction of all properties will pass through the market during a year, most have no recent market-established value. In its absence, assessments are relied upon with notoriously bad results.

The Bureau of the Census tabulates statistics which make the variability of assessment decisions glaringly evident. Only about 30% of all jurisdictions are able to maintain coefficients of dispersion[2] as low as 15%. As might be expected, places with less than 50,000 population have worse records than do larger cities and jurisdictions within an SMSA are more uniform than those outside (Table 4–3).

The meaning of a common level of dispersion for horizontal inequity can be made clear with a simple example. Assume that a jurisdiction is able to maintain a coefficient of 16%, that a sample of homeowners all have dwellings with a market value of $30,000, and that the effective tax rate is 2%. As Table 4–4 shows, the property tax burden might vary from $180 to $420.

1. In the New Haven region, for example, East Haven has had tax rates among the highest but has offered poor public services in return. Woodbridge and Orange, in contrast, have had both low taxes and excellent services.

2. The coefficient of dispersion is calculated as the sum of the absolute differences between actual and the median assessment ratios, divided by the number of properties, divided by the median ratio, multiplied by one hundred.

Table 4-3. Distribution of Selected Local Areas According to Coefficient of Dispersion of Assessment Ratios for Non-Farm Houses, by Types of Areas: 1966

| | | Percent of Areas | | | |
| | | *Area Population (1960)* | | *Selected Area Location Relative to SMSA* | |
Coefficient of Dispersion	*All Areas*	*>50,000*	*<50,000*	*Inside*	*Outside*
Total	100	100	100	100	100
0.0–10.0	7.6	4.4	9.8	9.8	6.1
10.0–14.9	20.6	25.8	17.0	29.6	13.9
15.0–19.9	25.2	30.6	21.6	28.8	22.6
20.0–24.9	15.7	15.9	15.6	11.6	18.7
25.0–29.9	11.3	11.3	11.4	9.1	13.0
30.0–39.9	9.8	6.7	11.9	5.2	13.1
40.0–49.9	5.5	3.5	6.8	2.9	7.4
50.0–more	4.3	1.8	6.0	3.0	5.2
Total Areas	1401	566	835	594	807

Source: U.S. Bureau of the Census, *Census of Governments, 1967.* Volume 2, Table 13.

Table 4-4. Variation in Property Taxes: An Hypothetical Example

Market Value	Assessed Value	Assessment Ratio (%)	Tax @ 2%	Deviation from Median Ratio
$30,000	$ 9,000	30	$180	-25
30,000	10,500	35	210	-20
30,000	12,900	43	258	-12
30,000	15,000	50	300	-05
30,000	15,300	51	306	-04
30,000	15,600	52	312	-03
30,000	16,500	55	330	0
30,000	17,100	57	342	+02
30,000	17,400	58	348	+03
30,000	18,000	60	360	+05
30,000	19,200	64	384	+09
30,000	20,100	67	402	+12
30,000	21,000	70	420	+15

Coefficient of Dispersion: 16%.

This example is, of course, hypothetical, but the variation in taxes is quite realistic; in Table 4-8 it can be seen that ratios of assessed to market values in the ten towns in the New Haven region vary from less than 30% to greater than 75%. Since family income is rather closely correlated with value of housing purchased, it seems that property taxes on residences are horizontally inequitable with respect to the usual standard.

Census figures may be used to indicate vertical inequity also. Price-related differentials for assessment ratios[3] indicate any tendency for the assessment ratio within a jurisdiction to vary systematically with the market value of the home. A differential of greater than one hundred indicates a tendency for higher-priced homes to have lower assessment ratios. While Table 4-5 shows that the majority of areas have no change in ratio, for nearly 40% of the jurisdictions studied, ratios decline with the value of the home. This could be interpreted as evidence of vertical inequity in property taxes on residences.

An additional source of apparent inequity is the practice of assessing different kinds of property at different proportions of market value (Table 4-5). Oldman and Aaron [31], for example, found that commercial property in Boston, sold in the period 1960-64, had an assessed value to sales price ratio of about 0.92; single family houses had a ratio of 0.38, while apartment houses for six or more families had a ratio of 0.63. In a recent study Black [7] has examined the variation in the pattern of assessment to sales price ratios for Boston even more closely. He finds also that ratios differ sytematically for different

3. The price-related differential is the result of dividing the mean assessment ratio for the area by the sales-based average assessment ratio. The latter is obtained by dividing the aggregate assessed value of the sold properties by the total of their sales prices.

Table 4–5. Distribution of Selected Local Areas According to Price–related Differential of Assessment Ratios for Non-farm Houses Within Each Area, by States: 1966

	Percent Having Price-related Differential of			
	-95.0	*95.0-104.9*	*105.0-119.9*	*120.0-*
U.S. (1401 areas)	2	59	32	7

Source: U.S. Bureau of the Census, *Census of Governments, 1967*. Volume 2, Table 17.

Table 4–6. Mean Assessment–Sales Ratios of Single–Family Properties by Population and Housing Characteristics

	1950	*1960*
All Census Tracts	0.54	0.39
Census Tract Characteristics		
Median Family Income		
Lowest 15%	0.69	0.53
Middle 70%	0.53	0.37
Highest 15%	0.44	0.35
Nonwhite Population Density		
Lowest 91%	0.53	0.37
Highest 9%	0.67	0.64
Density of Deterioration and Dilapidated Housing		
Lowest 85%	0.52	0.35
Highest 15%	0.65	0.58
Mean Owner Occupied Property Values		
Lowest 15%	0.57	0.46
Middle 70%	0.53	0.38
Highest 15%	0.56	0.38
Sample Size	101	94

Source: David E. Black, "The Nature and Extent of Effective Property Tax Rate Variation within the City of Boston," *National Tax Journal*, Vol. 25, No. 2 (June 1972), p. 206.

types of property. Of equal importance, the average assessment ratios for all types of properties vary systematically by location within the city. This aspect is illustrated for single family properties in the above Table 4-6. Here it appears that residential property in the poorest, blackest, most dilapidated and lowest average value tracts has a significantly higher average assessment ratio. Since blacks and the poor generally are more likely to live in higher–assessed multiunit dwellings than in single-family homes, and will usually live in the areas of higher average assessment ratios, the potential importance of the property tax as a cause of higher housing costs to disadvantaged persons seems quite great.

The Theory of Property Tax Capitalization

The statistics of the preceding section show that the property tax is an important source of revenue, particularly to local governments. They may also appear to demonstrate horizontal and vertical inequities, but this is by no means so evident as it seems. The basic question which must be resolved is, who actually pays the property tax? If, as one extreme case, taxes have been fully capitalized into location values, it cannot be inferred that present owners of high value houses are more favorably treated than present owners of low value homes even when it is known that assessment ratios in the jurisdiction decline as house values increase. In this case, the inequities would have been capitalized and borne by the owners of the property at the time the tax was initially imposed. For subsequent buyers, there would be no vertical inequity. A similar argument can be made for horizontal inequities arising from variable assessment ratios.

In addition to the problem of capitalization there are other reasons to feel uncertain what conclusions can be drawn from statistics like those of the previous section. For example, it is often said that the property tax is regressive because the ratio of house value to income falls as income rises. If true, this would seem to imply that even for jurisdictions where assessment to market price ratios are constant—and especially for those where the ratio falls—the tax is regressive. Leaving aside the possibility that house value relative to permanent income may be roughly constant, what this argument overlooks is that the property tax is not merely a tax on residential housing, it is a tax on capital throughout the economy. Because ownership of commercial and industrial property is concentrated in upper income brackets (and also because the assessment ratios for such property tend to exceed the ratios for residential property), the tax may well not be regressive.

What is necessary to make any progress in resolving these issues is better understanding of tax capitalization. Unfortunately, the theoretical guidance is not so precise as one could wish. At the very simplest level, it is generally agreed that a property tax on unimproved land cannot be shifted; it will be capitalized, reducing the market value of the land by the present value of the future tax obligations. But for a property tax on reproducible capital there is no concensus.

Mieszkowski [24] distinguishes three analytical positions.[4] The most commonly accepted view is that the property tax amounts to an excise tax on the use of capital. When each sector of the economy is viewed separately, it can be assumed that the supply of capital to that sector is elastic. Thus, it follows in

---

4. The best standard guide to the theory of property tax capitalization is Simon's classic review [42]. In a recent article Mieszkowski [24] has summarized, combined and significantly extended the previous analysis. What follows here will rely heavily on Mieszkowski's work.

the usual incidence analysis that the tax is shifted forward to consumers. This partial equilibrium analysis is the foundation for much empirical work related to the distribution of the tax burden by income class. Netzer has used it to calculate that property taxes on residential property are "equivalent to an excise tax of nearly 24% on rental value [of nonfarm housing in the United States] . . . " [29].

A second view, developed generally by Rolph and Break [39] and more specifically with reference to urban property taxes by Richman [36], holds that taxes on mobile capital will be borne by immobile resources, land in particular. In this view an increased property tax causes a site to have less net value to potential developers. To prevent their land from lying idle, landowners will find it necessary to absorb the property tax on both the bare land—as usually assumed—and the mobile capital. If they do not, development will occur where taxes are lower or nonexistent. A related possibility is that immobile workers might accept a cut in wages to retain the firm which employs them.

The third view is that the property tax on reproducible capital is approximately equivalent to a general profits tax [9]. The crucial assumption here is that capital is inelastically supplied to the economy as a whole; consequently, a reduction in the return will not alter the quantity offered and the owners of capital will bear the burden. This view emphasizes that property taxes are imposed throughout the economy. Therefore, it is incorrect to treat the tax on housing as an isolated excise tax which capital owners can avoid by shifting to other sectors.

Mieszkowski very neatly synthesizes these three alternatives, showing that there is some truth in each. Perhaps the key insight is the following:

> . . . excise tax effects will result from taxes imposed at varying rates on different types of property, or at varying rates in different regions or cities . . . [Yet] there is relatively little conflict between the view that property taxes are excises and the proposition that the basic effect of the property tax is to decrease the yield from real capital *if it is properly recognized that the global (nation wide) effects of the tax are quite different than the partial effects for a single city, or groups of cities.*
>
> From a national perspective the basic effect of the imposition of property taxes by thousands of local governments is to decrease the yield on reproducible capital. Relatively high tax rates in certain cities increase the prices of goods and services produced in these localities. However, these price increases will be tempered, even swamped, by decreases in the value of land and decreases in the returns to other imperfectly mobile factors of production. [24, p. 74]

Mieszkowski's analysis is directly applicable to the empirical design of the present study. Since the average global tax rate should act as a profits tax, we should not expect it to be capitalized into location value. Instead, we examine the effects of tax differentials which should act either as excise taxes (view one) or be capitalized into the returns to immobile factors (view two).

Yet even for tax differentials that should be capitalized, exactly what should be expected is not altogether certain. As Mieszkowski notes, the simplest expectation is that a tax differential will be fully capitalized into the value of land. Thus, if the tax differential for identical dwellings in New Haven and North Haven is $260 per year, and the rate of capitalization is 10%, the New Haven dwelling should sell for $2600 less than the North Haven dwelling. Mieszkowski, however, suggests two other possibilities. First, other immobile factors may exist and bear some burden. Specialized labor with work places in high-tax towns would possibly take a wage cut rather than see the employer move. Second, if the demand for land in high-tax towns is not price inelastic, an initial price decline from tax capitalization will induce substitution of land for other factors. This increased demand will temper the fall in price.

In the present case, however, neither of these latter possibilities is very likely. The metropolitan area is sufficiently small that specialized employment might easily move from a high-tax to a low-tax town without very greatly increasing the commuting cost of its labor force. Workers are unlikely to accept a wage cut to keep an employer in New Haven if the alternative location is North Haven. The question of substituting toward land as a production input becomes relevant to long-run analysis. However, with residential housing already constructed, substitution is unlikely to modify the decline in land values from initial capitalization.

In summary, the theory and empirical conditions in the region studied combine to suggest that if capitalization occurs, it will be of tax differentials only and should be reflected in location rents, not the returns to other immobile factors. If capitalization is not observed, the conclusion would seem to be that tax differentials act as excises on the consumption of housing services.

Tax Differentials in the New Haven Region and the Theory of Capitalization

The small size of the New Haven region, easy accessibility from one place to another, and varied housing stock within towns should, it would seem, be conducive to tax capitalization. Moreover, as Table 4-7 shows, effective tax rates among the ten towns of the New Haven region vary substantially. The high rate as a proportion of the low is 1.42, 1.60, and 1.52 for each of the years 1967, 1968, and 1969. Such differences are by no means trivial, for the annual tax payment on a $25,000 home in 1968 is increased by $260 if the home is moved from North Haven to New Haven. At plausible rates of capitalization such a tax differential should imply that homes in New Haven will be from $2,500 to $4,500 cheaper than identical homes in North Haven. Thus, the tax

Table 4-7. Tax Rates and Assessment Ratios

| Town | Assessment Ratio | | Effective Equalized Tax Mill Rates | | |
	Statutory	Actual	1967	1968	1969
Branford	0.66	0.47	22.09	22.09	22.09
Cheshire	0.60	0.50	22.00	23.75	20.25
East Haven	0.65	0.52	25.87	31.01	30.00
Hamden	0.60	0.53	19.03	21.20	23.21
New Haven	0.60	0.50	24.25	29.75	31.13
North Haven	0.55	0.47	19.36	19.36	20.49
Orange	0.60	0.50	18.25	20.25	23.25
Wallingford	0.60	0.50	23.50	25.50	27.50
West Haven	0.80	0.49	23.74	25.36	25.36
Woodbridge	0.50	0.46	20.70	23.23	25.21

Source: Statutory mill rates and assessment ratios taken from State of Connecticut, *Connecticut State Register and Manual 1969* (Hartford, 1969). The actual assessment ratio was calculated from the MLS sample. The effective equalized tax mill rate was calculated by applying the actual assessment ratio to the official mill rate.

effect is sizeable and unlikely to be submerged in random errors in the empirical analysis.

What these comparisons ignore, however, is the dual nature of the tax variations. As Table 4-8 shows, variations in the tax burden for a given housing bundle are as great within towns as between them. While the Census' coefficient of dispersion was not calculated, a somewhat similar measure is available: the standard deviation of the ratio of the sales price to the assessed value is in most of these towns 10% to 15% of the mean ratio and is occasionally greater. In part this variation reflects the vagaries of the assessment practices and in part the fact that general reassessments of each town occur only about every ten years; within this time changes in market conditions can substantially change the relative prices of different kinds of houses.

The previous review of national census statistics showed that intra-town differentials of the magnitude found in the New Haven region are by no means uncommon. Yet their importance for the process of tax capitalization has never been appreciated. Tax capitalization requires that potential buyers of each property perceive the tax obligations assumed with ownership. If two properties of equal market value carry unequal tax liabilities, tax capitalization can adjust the sales price to correct this difference, but the process requires that differentials be perceived.

Wide intratown tax differentials interfere in two ways. First, they create great uncertainty that tax differentials actually exist either between or within towns. Note, as one aspect of this, that even if the buyer is well informed, what he will know is the legal tax rate and the statutory assessment ratio. Actual assessment ratios are rarely close to the statutory, as Table 4-7 showed for the New Haven region, and they are almost never known to average citizens (except possibly for their own homes).

Table 4-8. Frequency Table for the Ratio of Assessed Value to Sales Price by Towns

Town	Assessed Value as a Percentage of Sales Price											
	20-25	25-30	30-35	35-40	40-45	45-50	50-55	55-60	60-65	65-70	70-75	75-80
Branford	0	1	4	14	15	10	7	0	1	0	0	0
Cheshire	0	0	4	7	30	59	48	24	5	3	0	0
East Haven	0	2	6	12	28	59	49	12	5	3	2	0
Hamden	0	0	1	19	32	89	122	101	37	11	5	0
New Haven	2	2	8	42	65	89	56	32	13	4	0	2
North Haven	0	3	16	42	67	49	27	11	2	2	0	0
Orange	0	0	2	12	20	38	34	14	5	1	0	0
Wallingford	0	1	3	22	43	31	11	2	0	0	0	0
West Haven	0	3	11	27	51	64	38	16	11	2	1	0
Woodbridge	0	0	4	15	26	32	10	1	0	1	0	0

Source: Records of the Multiple Listing Service.

One might suggest that buyers will ignore tax rates and statutory assessment ratios and simply compare the known tax liability of alternative dwellings. The wide intratown differentials interfere with capitalization in a second way at this point: large variations in property tax burdens will exist without legal sanction and no guarantee of continuing. Two households might purchase identical housing bundles in New Haven and Orange which because of errors in the assessment will have identical tax burdens despite the difference in tax rates. The household buying an underassessed home in New Haven would be foolish to pay much for that advantage, expecially shortly before general re-assessment is expected, because there can be no guarantee that the under-assessment will continue.

To summarize, two kinds of tax differentials exist: the legal differences between towns and the illegal differences within towns. Theories of tax capitalization have considered only the first of these. But illegal differences are as prevalent and as large as legal differences, and since illegal differences themselves are unlikely to be capitalized and furthermore tend to prevent capitalization of legal differences because of the confusion they create, the probability of observing tax capitalization is not so great as the simple calculation of legal tax differentials would imply. It is particularly important to emphasize that the assessment practices of the New Haven region studied are reasonably similar to those throughout the United States; thus similar problems exist generally, and the findings of this study should be widely applicable.

NEIGHBORHOOD EFFECTS

Approaches to Measurement
To say that locations offer different amenities and public services to their residents and that these differences will cause the values of structurally identical houses to differ is to say nothing particularly new. Nor is this an issue of scholarly concern only, as the well-known fear of the effect of racial integration on property values proves. Despite this, efforts to determine the importance of neighborhood effects in empirical analyses have had only limited success, reflecting the presence of severe difficulties both of conception and of practice. Perhaps the major stumbling block is the ill-defined and amorphous nature of the various neighborhood effects. Compared to brick siding, hardwood flooring, and copper plumbing, amenities such as congenial neighbors, good schools, and a safe neighborhood are vague and hard to quantify. Consequently, satisfactory measures to describe the variation of neighborhood amenities which the re-searcher observes have never been developed.

But the vagueness of most neighborhood amenities has an additional complicating effect. It is true of most commodities in most transactions that what the purchaser perceives himself as buying may differ from what an observer will perceive. Tawdry, vulgar products of all kinds doubtlessly are considered attractive and even elegant by those who purchase them. The importance of this problem would seem to be proportional in a sense to the vagueness of the commodity. For brick siding, hardwood floors, or copper plumbing objective measures and descriptions are relatively easy to establish, and reasonably good agreement can be expected between buyer and observer as to what was purchased. For safety, good schools, and congenial neighbors, objective measures are hard to establish; consequently, agreement between the buyer and the observer is less likely. In housing transactions the neighborhood amenity lies in the eyes of the purchaser, and the observer will have a difficult time determining this independently.

This difficulty has not, of course, been overlooked in previous studies of location characteristics. Oates, for example, commented that "*perceived benefits* [of education] in terms of smaller classes, better libraries, etc., . . . [are] what count in terms of the evaluation of different schools by parents" [30, p. 962]. Ridker and Henning, in a study of property values in St. Louis, argued that

> ideally, we should like to have information on *attitudes* about school quality and crime rates. . . . It should be clear without elaboration that subjective evaluations more directly determine property values. . . . [37, p. 249].

However, subjective evaluations by the purchasers of individual housing bundles have never been available, and this has made the problem of calculating reasonably acceptable measures of even ill-defined concepts like neighborhood safety imperative.

Previous studies have attempted to meet the challenge in several ways. Typically, the neighborhood effects are divided into what are called amenities, both natural and man-made, and public sector effects. The former includes such things as a pleasant view, clean air, the neighbors' well-manicured lawns and flower gardens, and the absence of barking dogs. The public sector effects are the results of government production of goods and services such as street cleaning, lighting, and maintenance, good or bad public schools, and police protection. The amenities of the neighborhood are then represented by proxies such as the average income and education level of neighborhood residents on the assumption that people of higher incomes and education will choose to live in attractive neighborhoods.[5] Any conclusions which are drawn from studies using such measures are, however, very questionable. Income and education will doubtlessly be correlated with the value of the housing units because of their roles in the demand function for housing; thus, no clear interpretation of any estimated coefficients is possible.

A much more ambitious attempt to measure neighborhood amenities

5. See, for example, [13], [30], [37].

is described in a recent paper by Kain and Quigley [17]. For each property, inspectors made thirty-two separate measures of such things as the character of the landscaping of the property and of the block in which it was located, the condition of curbs, sidewalks, and alleyways, and the amount of trash in sight. These measures were then combined by factor analysis to form measures of such things as the basic residential quality for each neighborhood. This procedure is certainly preferable to the use of income as a proxy for amenities; but, of course, there is no evidence that measures constructed in this way will rate neighborhoods as they are perceived by the residents.

After controlling in one way or another for the amenities of the neighborhood, the analyst must then attempt an equally difficult feat: measuring the output and quality of government services. For some simple government services, quite acceptable measures of output can be developed: pounds of garbage or sewage removed, gallons of water delivered per minute. But for even these, important quality variations exist that should ideally be recognized.[6] Other government programs have outputs that cannot be satisfactorily measured even when quality dimensions are ignored. What, for example, is a measure of police protection? Neighborhood crime rates are unsatisfactory measures because they take no account of any innate differences between neighborhoods in the generation of criminal actions. The appropriate measure would seem to be the number of crimes deterred, but crimes deterred are not easily counted.

Despite the difficulties, the urgent need for measures of public services has made efforts at measurement unavoidable. Two approaches have been taken: measurement of outputs, such as public protection or education, by the input of factors of production, which, being usually purchased at market prices, are easily measured; and heroic efforts to measure outputs directly. A common example of the latter is the comparison of the educational output of schools on the basis of the achievement test scores of pupils.

Neither measure is very satisfactory. Of comparisons of output which are based on measures of inputs, Margolis has written

> A larger expenditure figure is always an ambiguous number. Does a higher police expenditure per capita mean a greater preference for law and order via police services; or does it mean that the crime problem is greater and, therefore, the higher expenditures are needed to reach the same service level; or are the greater expenditures necessary because different urban forms make certain services more costly; or is there a shift in the composition of public and private provision of services? [22, p. 530-1]

Similar difficulties confound the interpretation of achievement

---

6. See, for example, Hirsch [15, p. 480] who distinguishes numerous qualities of garbage collection service depending on the frequency and place of collection.

scores as measures of educational output. What is desired is a measure of the ability of the school to impart knowledge and skills to pupils. Yet achievement scores reveal only what pupils can do and are silent on the school's role, since the pupil's ability, background, and other sources of information are not controlled.

Perceived Neighborhood Effects.

The inadequacies of most efforts to measure either the quantity or the quality of public services and the possibility that even acceptable objective measures of neighborhood effects will not correctly describe the neighborhood as it is seen by housing purchasers make the treatment of neighborhood effects in this study particularly interesting. Although some of the traditional measures of public service outputs will be used to describe neighborhood variations, the emphasis will be on the use of measures of perceived neighborhood effects.

From the discussion in Chapter Two it is clear that the value of neighborhood effects will depend upon the demands and the supplies *as perceived by purchasers.* Accordingly, the subjective evaluations of neighborhood effects were obtained from the survey of actual home-buyers discussed in the previous chapter. The relevant questions from that survey are shown in Table 4-9, where it can be seen that ratings of thirteen characteristics were requested

Table 4-9. Questions Regarding Perceived Neighborhood Amenities

Below is a list of some neighborhood characteristics. How would you rate the neighborhood you live in now regarding these? The numbers are a scale ranging from 1 (good) to 5 (bad). Please circle the number that best describes your feelings. If you don't know about something, please circle the A.

	Good				*Bad*	*Don't know*
Local elementary public school quality	1	2	3	4	5	A
Garbage collection service	1	2	3	4	5	A
Neighbors nearby	1	2	3	4	5	A
Ease of traveling to your job(s)	1	2	3	4	5	A
Street lighting, sweeping, and maintenance	1	2	3	4	5	A
Access to public parks and recreation	1	2	3	4	5	A
Ease of traveling to shopping areas	1	2	3	4	5	A
Local public high school quality	1	2	3	4	5	A
Convenience of bus service	1	2	3	4	5	A
	Little				*Much*	*Don't know*
Amount of heavy traffic on streets	1	2	3	4	5	A
Danger of fire nearby	1	2	3	4	5	A
Amount of air pollution	1	2	3	4	5	A
Danger of crime nearby	1	2	3	4	5	A

on an ordinal scale of 1 (good) to 5 (bad). The characteristics to be evaluated included such things as the quality of the local public elementary school, the amount of air pollution, the problem of heavy traffic on neighborhood streets, and the danger of crime; thus, the respondents were asked to evaluate both specific and rather general characteristics of the housing bundle they had purchased.

The initial step in constructing measures of neighborhood characteristics was the aggregation of individual household responses by single elementary school attendance boundaries and calculation of means for each question.[7] This procedure reflected two considerations. First, some way to define neighborhood areas was needed, and the elementary school boundaries seemed the best readily available approximations. There were roughly twice as many schools as census tracts—the obvious alternative—so school zones would on average be smaller and probably more homogeneous.[8] Of particular significance, aggregating by elementary school did not blur the evaluation of individual schools. This seemed desirable because for many purchasers it is likely that local school quality is the most important consideration in the evaluation of neighborhoods.[9]

But why, it may be asked, should one wish to use mean responses by neighborhood rather than responses of individual purchasers? Would it not be better to use what, after all, took much effort to collect? The consideration justifying the use of means is that means are likely to be a close approximation to the prevailing general judgments about neighborhood qualities and that these, rather than individual evaluations, will determine what must be paid for location characteristics in each neighborhood. This position is analogous to that reached in the discussion of land prices and accessibility in Chapter Two (Travel Times from the CBD), where it was suggested that persons working at minor employment centers away from the CBD may be able to live close to work without paying much for the great accessibility they obtain. To obtain locations close to work, the few local workers need only outbid the workers employed in the CBD for whom accessibility is low. Thus, to determine what part of the total sales price of the housing bundle is paid for accessibility, one must determine some measure of average accessibility at each location. Very wrong conclusions might be obtained if the price paid for each housing bundle were related to the accessibility enjoyed by the particular resident.

A similar argument applies to the effort to establish what part of the

7. In aggregating, I have excluded all blank and "don't know" responses.

8. There was no bussing for racial balance in this period.

9. There were two exceptions to the rule of aggregating evaluations by elementary school district. High schools received a score which was the average of all responses from the high school district. Ordinarily this would include many elementary school districts. Also, whenever there were fewer than four respondents per elementary school district, the responses were aggregated over a wider area, usually the census tract. The tract average was then taken as the score for the elementary school district.

Table 4-10. Correlations of Subjective Measures of
Neighborhood Quality

ELEMSC	1.00							
GARBGE	-0.12	1.00						
LIGHTG	0.13	0.57	1.00					
HIGHSC	0.82	-0.17	0.12	1.00				
TRAFIC	0.44	-0.17	-0.07	0.53	1.00			
FIRE	0.74	-0.11	0.27	0.63	0.51	1.00		
AIRPOL	0.67	-0.37	-0.02	0.77	0.63	0.65	1.00	
CRIME	0.79	-0.36	0.01	0.74	0.56	0.76	0.80	1.00

Definition of Variables
ELEMSC   Quality of local public elementary school
GARBGE   Quality of garbage collection
LIGHTG   Quality of street lighting, sweeping, and maintenance
HIGHSC   Quality of local public high school
TRAFIC   Amount of traffic on neighborhood streets
FIRE   Danger of fire
AIRPOL   Amount of air pollution
CRIME   Danger of crime

total price is paid for neighborhood amenities. Some persons may be attracted
to a neighborhood because they perceive its amenity level to be very high; but,
if this perception is not generally shared by other bidders, this household may
obtain the location at a much lower price than it would willingly pay. It reaps,
in other words, a consumer surplus. Similarly, a household may judge a neighborhood to be undesirable, but it will not for that reason be able to obtain the
location at less than what others will pay. Such considerations imply that using
individual evaluations of neighborhood amenity levels is less appropriate than
using the average of evaluations by all respondents in each neighborhood.

Five of the thirteen subjective evaluations were excluded from the
analysis for various reasons,[10] and preliminary investigations with the remaining
eight began. However, it was quickly apparent that the eight measures were too
highly correlated to be used individually, as is shown in Table 4-10.

This finding was not surprising. It is probable that when households
purchase a housing bundle, they evaluate the neighborhood in broader terms
than the specific measures they were asked to use in the questionnaire. Thus,
they may think of the neighborhood as being a more or less clean, safe and
pleasant place to live, rather than think specifically of the quality of garbage

10.Bus service was considered good in New Haven and poor elsewhere and
therefore served mostly as a town dummy variable. It was apparent from the use of
transit modes by respondents that bus service was not important to them. Access to shopping, jobs, and parks was usually judged good; and, in any case, accessibility enjoyed by
individual households is often irrelevant to location value for reasons given above. The
evaluation of neighbors was excluded because of some apparent misunderstanding by
respondents about what this meant.

collection, danger of crime, and amount of air pollution. Since all of the specific characteristics combine to define a clean, safe and pleasant neighborhood, the household's demands for each as a function of income, education, and other characteristics are likely to be similar. In response to the similar demands the qualities of various amenities provided within each neighborhood are likely to be similar.

Understandable though it might be, the substantial multicollinearity among the subjective evaluations required treatment before any clear interpretation of the location characteristics could be attempted. To reduce the problem of multicollinearity, I have applied the statistical technique of principal component analysis to the eight separate indices. The object of this method is to obtain linear combinations of the original variables of the sort

$$\xi_i = \sum_{j=1}^{P} \alpha_{ij} x_j, \qquad i = 1, \ldots, p \qquad (4\text{-}6)$$

where there are p original measures, the x's, from which are to be constructed p new variables, the principal components. The α_{ij}'s are chosen so that each ξ_i has as large a variance as possible, subject to the requirement that it must be uncorrelated with all preceding ξ_i's. Constructing the ξ_i's in this way, one finds that each successive component has a smaller variance than the previous ones. In favorable circumstances, it may be that the first few ξ_i's will account for most of the total variance of the original variables; if so, it may be possible to ignore the remaining components. The method has then permitted one to substitute a small number of uncorrelated indices of neighborhood amenities for the original larger number of correlated measures, yet most of the information of the original indices has been retained.[11]

Before considering the results of principal component analysis, it is necessary to evaluate one important objection to its use on a data set of subjective neighborhood qualities: is it appropriate to apply a technique which assumes cardinal data to a set of ordinal data? Principal component analysis deals with the correlation matrix for a set of variables, and it is well known that proper order–preserving transformations of ordinal data can very greatly change correlation patterns.

There are at least two defenses. Admitting the possibility that the components obtained are not invariant to scale changes, it can simply be said that the technique provides a convenient, though mechanical, way to combine partially interdependent measures. In this view no particular meaning should be attached to the components obtained.

11. For a more complete discussion of this technique see M.G. Kendall, *A Course in Multivariate Analysis* (New York: Hafner Publishing Co., 1968).

A second and much stronger defense than this is possible, however. While it is true that order-preserving transformations can distort a correlation matrix beyond recognition, there is a question of how bizarre such a transformation must be to achieve this end. Labovitz [20] has shown that the transformations most likely to create problems are those which convert a true cardinal scale of 1, 2, 3, 4 to 1, 9,998, 9,999, 10,000; that is, those which essentially dichotomize the sample. Other kinds of transformations leave correlation patterns quite similar. In particular, if the true cardinal rankings are monotonic and non-dichotomous, a simple linear, equal interval scale (1, 2, 3, 4) will be a good ordinal representation, in the sense that correlations between the two will be quite high (about 0.99). On the basis of his work, Labovitz concluded that a linear ordinal scale would provide a good approximation to a wide variety of true but unknown cardinal rankings and might appropriately be used to obtain correlations for relatively sophisticated statistical tests.

Since neighborhood qualities in the New Haven region seem to vary fairly continuously from good to bad, the equal interval scale used in the questionnaire should provide a reasonably good approximation to a true cardinal scale. The second defense, then, suggests that the principal component analysis can be used with some confidence. As will be seen, that confidence is greatly increased by the highly plausible results yielded.[12]

Proceeding now to the empirical results, principal component analysis of the eight measures of the subjective evaluation of location amenities revealed that more than three-quarters of the total variance could be accounted for by just two components. None of the remaining six components individually accounted for more than 8% of the total variance, nor, as will be explained, was it possible to interpret any of them. Accordingly, this study will use just the first two components to describe the variation in perceived neighborhood amenity levels.[13]

After using principal component analysis, one is faced with the problem of interpreting the individual components. Nothing guarantees that these will have an independent meaning, for they are merely statistical artifacts, a particular kind of linear combination of the original measures. The most common way to attempt interpretation of the components is to correlate them with the original variables, which has been done with the results shown in Table 4-11. The first component is highly correlated with six of the original variables: ELEMSC, HIGHSC, TRAFIC, FIRE, AIRPOL, and CRIME, and the second component with the remaining two; thus, the components distinguish what

12. The reader is, of course, free to accept the first defense only. No empirical results depend upon the components being anything more than convenient summaries of neighborhood qualities.
13. The decision to use only the first two components accords with the rule sometimes suggested of using only the components which have eigenvalues greater than 1.0, as the eigenvalue for the third component is 0.64.

Table 4–11.   Correlations of the First Two Components and the Original Variables

	Component 1	Component 2
ELEMSC	0.87	0.17
GARBGE	-0.32	0.84
LIGHTG	0.06	0.91
HIGHSC	0.88	0.10
TRAFIC	0.69	-0.10
FIRE	0.84	0.25
AIRPOL	0.89	-0.12
CRIME	0.92	-0.06

Eigenvalues for first two components: 4.45, 1.66
Percent of total variance accounted for: 76.4

Note: Responses were aggregated by individual elementary public school boundaries. The means calculated for each variable were used in this analysis.

appear to be two separate aspects of neighborhood quality. Because of the high correlation with variables which seem to measure "goodness of life" or "pleasantness of surroundings," I consider the first component to be a measure of the general quality of the neighborhood and refer to it as GEN Q. The second component, on the other hand, seems to reflect the provision of specific urban services. It will be named SERVCE.

To confirm the identification of the components, I have examined the scores attained by specific neighborhoods of the region. As one would expect, those areas favorably rated on the first component are high-income neighborhoods, not densely settled, with local reputations as pleasant places to live.[14] The badly rated neighborhoods are in poor, slum regions of New Haven. Similarly, the areas worst rated on the second component are parts of East Haven, which is notorious as a poor provider of public services.

In general, the densely populated, urban areas are rated rather favorably on the SERVCE component, whereas the suburbs are rated favorably on the GEN Q component. This result conforms remarkably well to the conventional dichotomy between the cities and the suburbs: cities have poor schools, heavy traffic, and crime problems, but they can do reasonably well at collecting garbage, cleaning streets, and providing sewerage; the suburbs, in contrast, enjoy good schools, little traffic, and little crime, but may provide only sporadic street maintenance and garbage collection.

Objective Measures of Neighborhood Effects.

To the extent that the demand for location is a function of perceived, not "real," neighborhood amenities, the use of subjective measures is highly

14. Recall that a high score (5) on the subjective evaluation indicated that the neighborhood was undesirable. Thus, a favorable rating corresponds to a low score. This is important to recall in evaluating the empirical results of Chapter 5.

appropriate. Nevertheless, it is of interest to consider also the use of some objective measures. Unfortunately only a few are available for this study. This results in part from the difficulties of putting together comparable data series from the official records of ten towns, in part from lack of needed data, and in part from uncertainty about what measures could appropriately describe some characteristics. Because of the importance of school quality to prospective buyers, according to anecdotal descriptions of the choice of residential location, particular emphasis was placed on obtaining measures of school quality. In addition, efforts were made to obtain measures of air pollution, crime, and fire danger, but with little success.

Two objective measures of school quality were obtained, both quite conventional. In an attempt to measure the school's ability to impart skills and information to the pupils, mean pupil achievement scores on standard reading tests were used.[15] These scores are probably not good measures of the school's ability to produce education because the quality and quantity of the inputs are not controlled. The lack of knowledge about children's native ability levels, backgrounds, and other possible sources of education is particularly grievous. Nevertheless, the scores may identify those schools which are thought to be good.

The second measure of school quality is the average pupil–teacher ratio in each public elementary school. In addition to whatever role this characteristic may play in determining the quality of the educational system, it is also a fairly good proxy for the expenditure per pupil in each school. Examination of these data, however, indicates that probably not much can be expected from them as measures of school quality. For most schools in most towns the ratio is about the same, approximately twenty–two to twenty–five pupils per teacher. More important, schools with lower ratios include those perceived as both good and bad. On the basis of the sample of schools in this study no firm conclusions can be reached; yet the evidence suggests that some schools are good possibly because they have low pupil–teacher ratios, whereas others have low ratios because they are bad. In the latter case adding teachers is one way to try to improve the school or halt further deterioration.

In addition to the objective measures of school quality, three objective measures of the provision of municipal services are included in this study. Not all cities in this region supply city water, city sewage disposal, or garbage collection to the residents. For housing bundles which lack municipal provision of these important services, purchasers will have to incur the cost of private provision from wells, septic tanks, and private rubbish haulers.

---

15. Four different tests were used in the various metropolitan schools: the Metropolitan, Stanford, Iowa, and California. Percentile scores on each of these were adjusted to be comparable. Pupil reading achievement is tested in different grades in various school systems, so the scores obtained are for pupils in either grade three or four. When possible, scores for different calendar years were averaged to eliminate random variation.

Comparison of Subjective and
Objective Measures

A question which arises naturally at this point is whether the subjective evaluations of neighborhood characteristics correspond to objective—or "true"—evaluations. Curiosity about this is probably inevitable, though it is somewhat idle. Given the great difficulties in establishing acceptable "true" measures of most neighborhood characteristics, it is not evident what one could conclude from observing that the two kinds of measures either agreed or disagreed. In any case, the paucity of objective measures available greatly restricts the comparisons which can be made. From the New Haven Bureau of Environmental Health, I have obtained fragmentary measures of the severity of air pollution within the city of New Haven.[16] As objective measures of school quality, average reading achievement scores of pupils in grades three to five are available.

These two measures permit some very limited comparisons of objective and subjective rankings. To do this, I have ranked observations first by one measure and then by the other and have then calculated the Spearman rank correlation coefficient between the two. For the twenty-eight census tracts in New Haven, the rank correlation for the measures of the severity of air pollution was +0.49, which exceeds the 5% two-tail critical value of 0.38 and therefore permits one to reject the hypothesis of independence. The correlation between the subjective and objective rankings of sixty-five school districts was even higher at +0.67 and also exceeds the 5% two-tail critical value of 0.36. These results may, perhaps, be reassuring to some either that households correctly recognize what is "true" or at least that what is measured in this fashion corresponds to what is perceived.

One additional useful comparison can be made between the subjective and objective measures. It has already been noted that the conventional central city-suburban dichotomy is apparent in the rankings by GEN Q and SERVCE: the suburbs offer good schools, clean air, and little crime, while the central city collects garbage well and cleans the streets. What is interesting is that these perceived differences may not correspond well to the "true" differences, objectively measured. I have previously shown that rank orderings of schools by perceived and objective measures of quality are highly correlated (+0.67); nevertheless, for some schools, and in some areas, quite striking differences in ranks exist. New Haven, for example, reputedly has a bad school system; and, indeed, most of its schools, as ranked by reading achievement scores, are the worst in the region. However, a few of its schools are good, and one had in recent years the highest average achievement test scores of any school for which there is information. The subjective evaluation of this school, nevertheless, ranks it below schools in Hamden which had achievement scores just slightly more than half as

16. New Haven Bureau of Environmental Health, "Air Pollution in New Haven," mimeo., 1970.

great. As another example, one school in Hamden and another in New Haven had almost identical achievement scores; but the former is subjectively ranked fourteenth among all schools, and the latter is ranked forty-first. Such differences reflect the fact that Hamden is thought to have good schools, and New Haven is not.

The implication of this finding is that flows of middle class families from New Haven to the suburbs cannot easily be slowed or halted when this movement is a result of fears about the adequacy of the school system. Policies may successfully maintain or restore "real" school quality in some schools without affecting the perceived quality. "Halo effects" give unjustified approval to poor schools in a town of generally good schools, and vice versa.

Chapter Five

The Prices of Components in the Housing Bundle

In Chapter Two "housing" was described as a heterogeneous bundle composed of three general kinds of commodities: Structural Characteristics, Location Characteristics, and Land. In every transaction of housing all of these components are purchased, but in differing amounts and qualities. Just as the purchase price of a bag of "groceries" depends on the particular items included—eggs, steak, and powdered milk—so the price of housing depends on the particular housing components purchased. The price of a house, then, can be given as

$$\text{Price} = \sum_{i=1}^{m} \alpha_i SC_i + \sum_{j=1}^{n} \beta_j LC_j + \gamma(D)L, \tag{5-1}$$

where:

SC_i is the ith structural characteristic and α_i the price per unit;

LC_j is the jth location characteristic and β_j the price per unit;

L is the quantity of land purchased and $\gamma(D)$ the price per unit, a function of of the accessibility of the location to the CBD.

Of course, the various prices for housing components are nowhere set out explicitly, as they are for foods in the supermarket; nevertheless, they are implicit in the transactions and can be expected to influence the purchases of each household.

In this chapter, the records of many housing transactions are analyzed, using the assumptions set out in Chapter Two, to determine estimates of the α's, β's, and γ. This is done in a very straightforward way by simply regressing the observed sales price of the total housing bundle on the various components included in the transaction.

THE VARIABLES

Structural Characteristics

The Structural Characteristics of the housing bundle include such things as the construction material, amount of insulation, the number of square feet of living area, the kinds of heating, plumbing, and electrical systems, overall quality, and numerous other special features. All the structural characteristics of the bundle which are included in the present analysis are listed and defined in Table 5-1.

Only a few points require comment. First, most of the structural characteristics of the housing bundle are described here by using dummy variables. Thus, HARDWD distinguishes houses which have all hardwood flooring from those which do not; and the group of insulation dummies—FULLIN, PARTIN, YESIN, and ROOFIN—distinguishes houses which have various amounts and kinds of insulation from those having none. To avoid creating a singular matrix in regressions where dummy variables are used, it is necessary always to omit one distinction from each exhaustive group of dummies. Thus, it is not possible to include, in addition to the preceding variables, dummies for such characteristics as SOFTWD (which would take the value 1 if the floor is not hardwood) or NOINS (which would take the value 1 if the house had no insulation). The value of the omitted dummy is incorporated in the regression intercept, and the values of those dummies included from each group are their values relative to the one omitted, not, in general, their absolute values. For example, the estimated price for HARDWD reveals the extra cost paid to have a hardwood floor rather than a floor of some other material, but it does not say what is paid to have a hardwood floor rather than no floor at all. Only when the variable omitted from each group is the one identifying the houses lacking some features are the estimated values for the included variables both relative and absolute values. This, for example, is true of the set of insulation variables, since the omitted variable is NOINS.

Because the values of omitted dummy variables are incorporated in the constant term, this will have a particular meaning in the present analysis. Specifically, the constant term can be interpreted as the value of a house of overall good quality, made of wood, with wood shingles or other wood facing, not insulated, with softwood or tile floors, no basement, one full bathroom, no partial baths, no basement laundry, galvanized plumbing, a 110 volt electrical system handling less than 75 amperes, a forced air or electrical heating system, one adjustable heating zone, no fireplace, and neither garage nor carport.

The second point for comment is that in equation (5-1) the individual components enter additively, and, thus, the contribution of each to the total

Table 5-1. Structural Characteristics in the Housing Bundle

FACBSS	Dummy variable taking value of 1 if house is made of brick, stone, or stucco, or has these materials used as facing. $(R)^a$
FACASB	Dummy variable taking value of 1 if house has asbestos shingle facing. (R)
FULLIN PARTIN YESIN ROOFIN	Dummy variables taking value of 0 or 1 if structure has, respectively, full insulation, partial insulation, insulation but amount not specified, or insulation in roof only. $(S)^a$
SQFT SQFT 2	Number of square feet and square feet squared of living space in house in thousands of feet.
ROOM/S	Number of rooms in house, including any finished basement rooms, divided by thousands of square feet.
HARDWD	Dummy variable taking value of 1 if house has all hardwood flooring. (S)
EXCLNT V GOOD FAIR	Dummy variables taking value of 1 if this is the realtor's description of overall quality. (S)
BASMNT	Dummy variable having value of 1 if house has a basement.
BATHS	Number of full bathrooms in house less one.
PBATHS	Number of partial bathrooms in house.
LANDRY	Dummy variable taking value of 1 if basement includes a laundry area with drains and spigots.
PLUMBR	Dummy variable taking value of 1 if plumbing is all of copper or brass. (R)
220VLT	Dummy variable taking value of 1 if house is wired for 220 volt appliances.
75+AMP	Dummy variable taking value of 1 if house has wiring to supply more than 75 amperes.
STEAM RAD HT	Dummy variables taking value of 1 if house has, respectively, steam or hot water radiant heat. (S)
ZONES	Number of individually adjustable heating zones less one.
FIREPL	Number of fireplaces.
SPLIT STORY2	Dummy variables taking value of 1 if house is, respectively, a split level or two story structure.
CARPRT GAR1 GAR2	Dummy variables taking value of 1 if house includes, respectively, a carport, a one-car garage only, or a two or more car garage.
TIME*S TIM2*S	Time trend—the number of months and months squared from January 1967 until the date of sale. (S)
AGE*S AGE2*S	Age and age squared of house in decades at time of sale. (S)
PRICE	Total sales price of housing bundle in thousands of dollars.

[a](R) or (S) following the definition of a variable indicates that the variable has been multiplied by the square root of the number of square feet of living space or by the number of square feet.

sales price is independent of all others. Since the functional form implies an absence of interdependencies, those thought to exist must be recognized by defining the variables appropriately. For example, it is more expensive to insulate a large house fully than a small one, so one would expect the price differential between fully insulated and uninsulated houses to increase with the size of the house. Consequently, the appropriate independent variable for (5-1) is not a simple dummy for full insulation, but rather one which describes the area that is fully insulated. All the insulation dummies have accordingly been scaled by multiplying them by SQFT. Similar considerations applied to many of the variables in Table 5-1, and scaling is indicated by and "S" or "R" in parentheses following the definition.

The reader will note that AGE and TIME were both scaled by SQFT; but the rationale in these cases was slightly different than for other variables. Scaling of these variables was required because it seemed likely that the depreciation due to age and appreciation due to inflation would cause price changes in each time period proportional to total price. A simple time trend in (5-1) would, however, imply equal absolute price changes for all bundles regardless of their total cost. Consequently, it would seem desirable to scale the time trend by the sales price of the total bundle. This intuitively appealing adjustment was not possible, however, because it would introduce a correlation between the independent variables and the error term in (5-1) that would bias the estimated coefficients. The simplest resolution of the problem was to use SQFT as the scaling factor because of its high simple correlation with price (+0.75).

Finally, the interior space of the dwelling is described in this study with two variables, SQFT and ROOM/S. The size of a dwelling is usually, and appropriately, measured by the square feet of living area. But SQFT alone is insufficient to describe the roominess, separation of family activities, and privacy available to family members; it matters, too, how the interior space is divided into parts. ROOM/S is intended to capture this second aspect, as a measure of interior spaciousness.

Land Prices

The theoretical discussion of land prices in Chapter Two concluded that the price of land in each location in a metropolitan region would reflect, among other things, the cost of transportation from the site to centers of economic activity. Transportation costs were assumed to be a function of vehicle operation costs and the time costs of travel; but by making the simplifying, and fairly plausible, assumption that the transportation system permitted equally rapid travel in all directions from the CBD, it was possible to make transportation costs a function of only the distance traveled. Thus, the price of land could be written as

$$P_L = \alpha + \beta f(D), \qquad (5-2)$$

and the total expenditures for land in the housing bundle as

$$P_L L = \alpha L + \beta f(D)L. \tag{5-3}$$

In the empirical analysis presented in this chapter, equation (5-3) is augmented by a term, γL^2, to permit economies of scale in the purchase of large quantities of land:

$$P_L L = \alpha_L + \beta_f(D)L - \gamma L^2. \tag{5-4}$$

Such economies could arise for several reasons: surveying, titling, and selling costs for land probably do not rise proportionately with size; assessments for municipal improvements commonly are based on frontage rather than lot size; and, most importantly, large lots are likely to be qualitatively different from small ones. Lots of an acre or more are not likely to be sodded, planted, or fenced as intensively as are smaller lots. In the absence of controls for such quality variations, there will appear to be economies of scale.

For the empirical analysis of this chapter the general accessibility function $f(D)$ in equation (5-4) must be replaced with some specific function. Two are chosen for close examination, the inverse function and the natural logarithm function. Both imply that land prices fall nonlinearly with distance, as seems reasonable in this analysis. Since distance here is a proxy for both vehicle operation costs and time costs, a linear function would be appropriate only if the rate of speed remained constant as the distance traveled increased. However, as shown in Chapter Two (Travel Times from the CBD), speeds on radials from the CBD increase markedly with distance; therefore, time costs per mile traveled will fall with distance and so may vehicle operation costs, since automobiles are more efficient when they operate at high speeds without having to stop frequently.

In addition to the two functions which relate land prices to the distance from the CBD, I have examined one simplified variant of the employment gravity model, as described in Chapter Two (Land Rent Gradient). This function measures the accessibility of each location in terms of the distance to the CBD and to the industrialized northwest corner of tract 38, and weights the distance to each center by the employment there. The specific formula is

$$\text{Access} = E_1/D_1 + E_{38}/D_{38} \tag{5-5}$$

where

E_1 is the number of jobs in the CBD;

E_{38} is the number of jobs in the industrialized portion of tract 38;

Table 5-2. Variables Used in Determining Land Value

SIZLOT	Lot size in tens of thousands of square feet.
SIZLT2	Lot size in tens of thousands of square feet squared.
INVDST	Inverse of distance in miles from New Haven Green multiplied by SIZLOT.
LDST*A	Natural logarithm of distance in miles multiplied by SIZLOT.
GRAVTY	Inverse of distance from New Haven Green weighted by employment (in thousands of jobs) in tracts 1, 2, 3, 17 (21.331 thousands of jobs) plus inverse of distance from industrial area in tract 38 weighted by employment there (3.071 thousands of jobs). $GRAVTY = 21.331/D_1 + 3.071/D_{38}$
LGRAV	Natural logarithm of GRAVTY.
LGRV*A	LGRAV multiplied by SIZLOT.
MINITS	Travel time in minutes from New Haven Green multiplied by SIZLOT.

Note: All distances were measured from the edge of the New Haven Green at the corner of Church and Chapel Streets (Tract 1) to the middle of the tract in which the house is located, except for the large tracts (37, 38, 39, 40, 41) which were further subdivided.

D_1 is the distance from the tract in which the house is located to tract 1;

D_{38} is the distance from the tract in which the house is located to the industrial portion of tract 38.

The gravity measure will be tested both as calculated by equation (5-5) and in a logarithmic transformation.

Out of interest, travel time rather than distance traveled will also be examined as an argument in the accessibility function in equation (5-4). Since the travel time naturally allows for the increasing speed with greater distance, no nonlinear transformation of travel time is required.

All the variables which will be used in the empirical analysis of land prices are listed and defined in Table 5-2.

The Location Characteristics

The Location Characteristics to be examined include accessibility, subjective and objective measures of neighborhood quality, property tax differentials, and certain public services. Since the values placed on these are of keen interest and the measurement problems most severe, they have all been discussed fully in the preceding chapters. A complete list, including brief definitions, is found in Table 5-3.

There is one remaining general issue which requires comment: Should the contribution of a locational amenity to the sales price be a lump sum or should it be related to the quantity of land purchased? For many amenities, including a scenic view, quiet garbage collection, and the right to send children

Table 5-3.   Location Characteristics

TAXDIF	Excess property tax liability in thousands of dollars, calculated as $(r_a \cdot AV - r_L \cdot AV)$
	where r_a = mill rate in town where property is located
	r_L = mill rate in low tax reference town (North Haven)
	AV = assessed value of property
PRCNTL	Average percentile score of students at the local public elementary school in 3rd or 4th grades on reading achievement tests.
STRTIO	Student–teacher ratio at the local public elementary school 1967–70.
GEN Q	Score of the neighborhood (defined by elementary school districts) on the first principal component of purchasers' subjective evaluation of neighborhood.
SERVCE	Score of the neighborhood on the second principal component.
RGEN Q	Residual from regression of GEN Q on TAXDIF.
RSRVCE	Residual from regression of SERVCE on TAXDIF.
RGENQ%	Residual from regression of GEN Q on PRCNTL.
CWATER	Dummy variable taking value of 1 if city supplies water.
CSEWER	Dummy variable taking value of 1 if city provides sewerage.
GARBGE	Dummy variable taking value of 1 if the city collects garbage.

to a superior public school, benefits are apparently unrelated to the quantity of land occupied. This suggests that the household would bid a lump sum for the privileges.

But consider the decision of a developer of vacant land. If his location enjoys a fine view, households will pay extra to live here. To maximize profits, the developer must select an optimal lot size; the smaller the lots, the more houses he will have available to sell at a premium. Consequently, a buyer wanting a double-sized lot must be prepared to pay the location premium for both small lots. Otherwise, the developer will prefer a sale to a second household. This suggests that payments for amenities will be proportional to lot size.

It is difficult to resolve this question for many reasons; zoning restrictions, topographical irregularities, and the fact that we deal with sales of existing properties where lot size adjustment is generally impossible, are only a few of the nonmarket complications. The choice made—purely for statistical convenience—was to treat payments for amenities as lump sums. While not presented below, alternative calculations with the opposite assumption yielded very similar results.

ESTIMATED PRICES

Estimated market prices for the various components of the housing bundle have been obtained by regressing the sales price of each house on the Structural Characteristics, Location Characteristics, and the amount of Land purchased in that transaction. The method and assumptions of ordinary least squares regression analysis (OLSQ) are well-known and will not be discussed here,[1] particularly since the present analysis was quite straightforward and encountered few econometric difficulties. There are, however, a few points which require comment before the estimated prices are presented.

First, to estimate the coefficients in equation (5-1), it was necessary to assume that it could be rewritten as

$$Price = \alpha SC + \beta LC + \gamma(D)L + U. \tag{5-6}$$

where the variables are vectors of the prices and characteristics defined in (5-1). The additional term, U, is a vector of random disturbances, assumed to be distributed normally with zero mean and constant variance σ^2. The assumption of constant variance for the error term is necessary in regression analysis for the estimated prices to be *best* linear unbiased estimates. If the error term has a non-constant variance, the estimates will not be biased, but they will be inefficient.[2]

Preliminary investigations indicated that for the present analysis, the assumption of homoscedasticity was not tenable: plots of the residuals from regressions in the form of equation (5-6) revealed that the variance of the residuals increased markedly with the size and price of the house. Correct treatment of heteroscedasticity requires that a transformation matrix Λ be obtained which has the characteristic

$$E(\Lambda UU'\Lambda') = \sigma^2 I. \tag{5-7}$$

Then, if equation (5-6) is premultiplied by this matrix, the resulting equation will be homoscedastic, as required.

Finding the correct transformaton matrix is ordinarily not easy; however, the residual plots indicated that an approximately correct treatment of heteroscedasticity could be achieved by assuming that the standard deviation of the error term in (5-6) is proportional to SQFT. If

$$u_i = SQFT_i \sigma_i, \qquad i = 1, \ldots, k \tag{5-8}$$

then

$$\frac{u_i}{SQFT_i} = \sigma_i. \qquad i = 1, \ldots, k \tag{5-9}$$

---

1. Techniques and assumptions of multivariate regression analysis are discussed in any textbook of econometric methods. See, for example, J. Johnston, *Econometric Methods* (New York: McGraw-Hill Book Company, Inc., 1963).
2. Johnston, *Econometric Methods*, p. 209.

Table 5-4. Estimated Prices for Structural Characteristics

Variable	Coefficient	t-value	Variable	Coefficient	t-value
INTERCEPT	2.93	(2.84)	LANDRY	0.33	(1.58)
FACBRK (*R*)	1.08	(4.35)	SPLIT	0.64	(3.14)
FACASB (*R*)	-0.77	(1.68)	STORY2	0.43	(2.00)
FULLIN (*S*)	0.94	(3.79)	CARPRT	0.16	(0.38)
PARTIN (*S*)	0.22	(0.65)	GAR1	0.78	(4.07)
YESIN (*S*)	0.69	(3.24)	GAR2	2.46	(9.83)
ROOFIN (*S*)	0.48	(1.16)	TIME*S (*S*)	0.071	(2.44)
SQFT	5.20	(5.77)	TIM2*S (*S*)	0.001	(1.61)
SQFT2	1.03	(4.49)	AGE*S (*S*)	-1.38	(11.79)
ROOM/S	0.64	(8.17)	AGE2*S (*S*)	0.09	(6.83)
HARDWD (*S*)	0.72	(3.89)	PLUMBR (*R*)	0.07	(0.17)
EXCLNT (*S*)	1.29	(6.69)	220VLT	0.63	(2.03)
V GOOD (*S*)	0.53	(2.32)	75+AMP	0.41	(2.45)
FAIR (*S*)	-1.27	(2.56)	STEAM (*S*)	0.77	(3.06)
BASMNT	0.61	(2.28)	RADHT (*S*)	0.23	(1.70)
BATHS	2.56	(11.50)	ZONES	0.53	(2.42)
PBATHS	1.11	(6.02)	FIREPL	1.11	(6.99)

Notes:
Dependent variable is PRICE.
Scaling by SQFT or square root of SQFT is indicated by (*S*) or (*R*) following the variable name.
Figures in parentheses are *t*-statistics with approximately 1,850 degrees of freedom. For most variables, a one-tail test is appropriate. Accordingly, a value of 2.32 (1.28) indicates significance at the 1(10) percent level.

Thus, by dividing all variables in each observation by SQFT, it was possible to obtain a new equation in which the disturbance term has the desired homoscedastic form. This treatment of heteroscedasticity was, of course, somewhat crude because of the simple assumption in (5-8); nevertheless, plots of residuals from the transformed model indicated that the assumption eliminated obvious evidence of heteroscedasticity and was better than any other simple assumption.[3]

To avoid misunderstanding, I should mention that no allowance for the treatment of heteroscedasticity is necessary in the interpretation of the estimated prices given in Tables 5-4 and 5-5. That is, the coefficient for BASMNT is the estimated price for BASMNT and not for BASMNT/SQFT, even though the coefficient was obtained in a regression which used the latter variable and not the former.[4]

The treatment for heteroscedasticity does, however, affect the interpretation of some of the summary statistics. In particular, the standard

3. A weaker correction for heteroscedasticity was also tested in which the variance of the error term was assumed proportional to SQFT. Residual plots indicated that this correction was insufficient.

4. See Johnston, *Econometric Methods*, p. 211.

Table 5-5. Taxes, Services, Amenities, and Accessibility

Variable	Regression (1)		Regression (2)		Regression (3)		Regression (4)		Regression (5)		Regression (6)	
CWATER	-0.39	(1.35)	-0.39	(1.35)	-0.48	(1.65)	-0.44	(1.49)	-0.46	(1.57)	-0.50	(1.71)
CSEWER	0.50	(2.49)	0.50	(2.49)	0.62	(3.09)	0.55	(2.72)	0.58	(2.89)	0.62	(3.07)
GARBGE	0.38	(1.55)	0.38	(1.55)	0.87	(3.67)	0.61	(2.37)	0.49	(1.92)	0.62	(2.48)
TAXDIF	-0.22	(0.18)	-0.22	(0.18)	-0.45	(0.36)	-0.15	(0.12)	-0.40	(0.32)	-0.49	(0.40)
GEN Q	-1.37	(7.85)	-1.37	(7.85)	-1.20	(5.58)	-1.47	(7.38)	-1.31	(7.47)	-1.25	(7.19)
SERVCE	-0.36	(3.83)	-0.36	(3.83)	-0.23	(2.45)	-0.26	(2.75)	-0.30	(3.16)	-0.27	(2.89)
SIZLOT	1.70	(9.80)	0.44	(3.15)	0.90	(8.78)	0.91	(8.89)	0.32	(1.70)	1.17	(8.01)
SIZLT2	-0.01	(2.33)	-0.01	(2.43)	-0.02	(3.52)	-0.02	(3.57)	-0.01	(2.63)	-0.02	(3.12)
LDST*A	-0.46	(5.68)										
INVDST			2.37	(4.70)								
GRAVTY					-0.02	(0.45)						
LGRAV							0.65	(2.25)				
LGRAV*A									0.38	(3.58)		
MINITS											-0.02	(2.61)
					Summary Statistics							
R²	0.73		0.72		0.72		0.72		0.72		0.72	
F-value	116.17		115.31		113.44		113.85		114.51		114.00	
S.E.E.	2.65		2.65		2.67		2.67		2.66		2.67	
d.f.	1849		1849		1849		1849		1849		1849	

The Prices of Components in the Housing Bundle 77

Variable	Regression (7)		Regression (8)		Regression (9)		Regression (10)		Regression (11)	
CWATER	-0.39	(1.34)	-0.22	(0.65)	-0.15	(0.50)	-0.26	(0.79)	-0.26	(0.79)
CSEWER	0.50	(2.48)	0.64	(2.54)	0.22	(1.06)	0.88	(3.46)	0.88	(3.46)
GARBGE	0.38	(1.55)	0.05	(0.15)	-0.06	(0.24)	0.23	(0.71)	0.23	(0.71)
TAXDIF	-6.03	(5.63)	-2.85	(2.21)	-5.59	(4.63)	-0.53	(0.38)	-0.53	(0.38)
GEN Q							-0.97	(4.42)		
SERVCE	1.69	(9.80)	-0.40	(3.42)	-0.46	(4.60)	-0.37	(3.18)	-0.37	(3.18)
SIZLOT	-0.01	(2.33)	1.69	(8.89)	1.40	(7.44)	1.66	(8.78)	1.66	(8.78)
SIZLT2	-0.46	(5.67)	-0.01	(2.29)	-0.02	(3.16)	-0.01	(2.11)	-0.01	(2.11)
LDST*A	-1.37	(7.84)	-0.45	(5.02)	-0.23	(3.16)	-0.46	(5.08)	-0.46	(5.08)
RGEN Q	-0.36	(3.83)								
RSRVCE										
PRCNTL			0.03	(6.72)	0.03	(0.91)	0.02	(3.97)	0.04	(7.96)
STRTIO										
RGENQ%									-0.97	(4.42)
Summary Statistics										
R^2	0.73		0.72		0.72		0.72		0.72	
F-value	116.15		94.64		110.78		93.99		93.99	
S.E.E.	2.65		2.71		2.65		2.69		2.69	
d.f.	1849		1506		1760		1505		1505	

Figures in parentheses are t-statistics with approximately 1,850 degrees of freedom. For most variables a one–tail test is appropriate. Accordingly, a value of 2.32 (1.28) indicates significance at the 1(10) percent level.

error of estimate, the R-square for the regression, and the F-value refer to the homoscedastic model estimated rather than to the original heteroscedastic model. Thus, the standard error is in dollars per square foot although the dependent variable for the original model is the total sales price. This reflects the assumption that the error increases with the size of the house. The R-square calculated describes the ability of the model to explain the variation in the transformed dependent variable PRICE/SQFT rather than the original PRICE. Much of the explanatory power of the original model depends on the high correlation of PRICE and SQFT. The transformation to new variables eliminates this, and the R-square is consequently reduced. As an indication of the true R-square for the original model, I have calculated the squared simple correlation of PRICE and predicted PRICE using the coefficients in Tables 5-4 and 5-5, Column 1. In comparison to the R-square of 0.72 calculated for PRICE/SQFT, the R-square for PRICE is about 0.85.

Since the F-statistic for the test of the goodness of fit for the regression as a whole can be written in terms of R-square,[5] the incorrect R-square caused the F-statistic to be incorrect also; in particular, the F-statistic is too small. It is, nevertheless, highly significant, and since the hypothesis it tests is of limited interest, I have made no effort to correct it.

The second point requiring brief comment is the possible problem of multicollinearity. It may be supposed that in regressions using forty or more independent variables the correlations among many of the variables will necessarily be large so that the separate influences of each cannot be identified. In general, however, this is not so. In Chapter Two (Small Area Variation of Housing Bundles), it was mentioned that, at the level of disaggregation used in this study, substantial variation in the composition of the housing bundle was possible. As expected, the simple correlations among twelve of the variables, presented in Table 2-4, were rarely greater in absolute value than 0.2.[6] Furthermore, the larger correlations were usually the result of my having scaled some variables by SQFT. This, for example, is the explanation for the correlation of +0.6 between HARDWD and SQFT. The correlation between the hardwood floor dummy unscaled and SQFT is almost zero. Similarly, the division of all independent variables by SQFT as a correction for heteroscedasticity tended to intensity whatever natural correlations existed among the independent variables. Inspection of a table of simple correlations among the transformed variables would uncover some correlations greater than 0.8 in absolute value, but they can be traced to the correction made for heteroscedasticity. Because multicollinearity does not itself cause the least squares estimates of properly specified models to

5. $F = R^2/(k - 1) \, / \, (1 - R^2)/(n - k)$ for k variables and n observations.

6. However, knowledge that simple pair–wise correlations are small does not necessarily rule out the possibility that groups of variables will be perfectly correlated, as Kmenta shows [19, p. 383]. Yet the stability of estimates regardless of what variables are included or excluded suggests that this is not a major problem.

be biased, and because much of the observed correlation among variables is, in a sense, spurious—the result of scaling by a common factor—the accuracy of the estimated coefficients should not, in general, be impaired. Moreover, the large number of observations helps to insure that the estimates have small standard errors.

A third point for comment is whether or not it is correct to apply an ordinary least squares regression to (5-6). One assumption of this method is that the right-hand variables are not determined jointly with the left-hand variable; they must, that is, be either exogenous or predetermined. If the dependent and independent variables are determined jointly in a simultaneous equation system, then the error term in (5-6) will be correlated with the independent variables, and applying OLSQ to the single equation will yield biased estimates of the coefficients.[7]

The possibility of simultaneous determination arises in this study with respect to the neighborhood amenities, since it can be argued that taxes, house values, and expenditures on public services are all interdependent [30, p. 964]. Given the expenditure levels and the house values, the amounts to be collected from property taxes on each house are largely determined; given the tax bill and provision of services, the value of a particular bundle of housing services is determined.

The argument that house values, taxes, and public services should be regarded as simultaneously determined appears, however, to be unimportant with respect to the present study. This follows from an institutional characteristic of assessment practices in the New Haven region which tends to reduce the simultaneity between taxes and house values, given the levels of neighborhood services, however measured. Specifically, general reassessment of all houses in relation to market value occurs infrequently, thus holding the tax base constant regardless of changes in taxes which might be capitalized into market value. Except in the long run, the feedback of reductions in market value in response to tax increases which necessitate further tax adjustments is avoided. If, as is customary in some areas, houses were routinely reassessed after each sale, the simultaneity would be a more serious problem.

The force of institutional practice in the region is, I believe, very greatly to weaken the arguments in favor of regarding neighborhood characteristics, house values, and taxes as simultaneously determined. In the short run that characterizes each decision to buy it seems quite appropriate to take the neighborhood characteristics, including taxes, as predetermined, which makes the use of OLSQ regressions acceptable. Doubtlessly, in a study of housing values over time more attention to this point would be necessary.

Finally, a few words about Tables 5-4 and 5-5 will make the entries clearer. Table 5-4 contains the estimated prices for the Structural Characteristics

7. See Johnston, *Econometric Methods,* Ch. 9.

of the housing bundle, and Table 5-5 contains the prices for Land and Location Characteristics. It will be noticed, however, that only one set of estimates for Structural Characteristics is given, while many sets of prices for Land and Location Characteristics are presented. The explanation for this is quite simple: although each regression included measures of all Structural and Location Characteristics and Land as independent variables, the prices estimated for Structural Characteristics were essentially the same in each regression. To save space, and because these prices are relatively unimportant in this study, I have not reported the coefficients for the Structural Characteristics from regressions (2) to (11). Thus, regression (1) is the only one for which all results are reported: the prices of Structural Characteristics are in Table 5-4, and the prices of Land and Location Characteristics are in Column 1, Table 5-5.

Prices of Structural Characteristics

Not too much needs to be said about the estimated prices of Structural Characteristics given in Table 5-4; for some purposes they are highly useful, but here their main value is as benchmarks to judge the plausibility of the estimation results. On purely statistical grounds, the coefficients are generally quite satisfactory: most values are significant at the 1% level and have the anticipated signs. Judging how reasonable they are as hedonic prices is more difficult except in a few cases.

The annual percentage rates of inflation implied by TIME*S and TIM2*S are 5.4, 6.6, and 7.5 for each of the years 1967, 1968, and 1969.[8] These rates compare closely to the rates of change of 4.2, 6.4, and 7.3 in the "Housing" price index from the *Survey of Current Business.*[9] The coefficients for AGE*S and AGE2*S imply that a twenty-five year old house of 1.4 thousand square feet will sell for $4,040 less than an identical new house. This decline in value is similar to, but somewhat greater than, the $3,150 reduction which Kain and Quigley found in St. Louis for an equally old house [17, p. 539]. But, since the market structure and kinds of houses differ between these two cities, one should perhaps be as surprised by close agreement as by differences. One other easy comparison is possible: the estimated price of $1,110 for a fireplace is quite close to what is charged by many builders for this feature. Cost-of-construction comparisons are open also for HARDWD, BATHS, PBATHS, GAR1, and GAR2. In each case, the estimated values seem plausible.

8. These rates of inflation were calculated by applying the coefficients for TIME*S and TIM2*S to a house selling for $25,000 in January 1967, and having 1.4 thousand square feet of living area. Both the price and the size are approximate sample means.

9. U.S. Department of Commerce, *Survey of Current Business* (Washington, D.C.: Government Printing Office, various issues). The index of "Housing" prices is based on more than changes in the selling prices of single-family homes, and the comparisons made are, therefore, not entirely correct.

One could continue to judge how reasonable the various estimated structural prices are, using construction costs as measures for comparison or relying on simple *a priori* considerations; but, given the limited importance of these prices in this study, this would have little value.

Land Prices and Accessibility

In this study, the effect of accessibility on land prices was investigated using several different measures to replace the general function $f(d)$ in equation (5-4). Preliminary results indicated that, if distance from the CBD were used as the measure of accessibility, a linear function would be inappropriate. This finding accorded with the expectations expressed in the Land Prices Section (p. 70) of this chapter that, because of the marked increase in the speed of travel as distance from the CBD increased, time costs and even some mechanical costs of travel would decline per unit distance traveled. The change in speed with distance implied that land prices would decrease rapidly at first and then more slowly as distance from the CBD increased. Consequently, the measures of accessibility which I have used are nonlinear in distance.

The first function I have used to examine the effect of accessibility on land value is the natural logarithm of the straight-line distance to the CBD. The rate of decline of land values with distance is indicated by the coefficient of LDST*A in Table 5-5, Column 1, and some sample land values at various distances from the CBD are given in Table 5-6, Columns 1 and 2. The estimated coefficients for all the variables in equation (5-4) are highly significant, statistically; nevertheless, there is some quesiton whether the equation correctly

Table 5-6. Estimated Land Values

	Accessibility Measured by			
	*LDST*A*		*INVDST*	
Miles from Center	*Price[a] (1)*	*Relative Price (2)*	*Price[a] (3)*	*Relative Price (4)*
0.5	2.01	1.19	5.17	1.85
1.0	1.69	1.00	2.80	1.00
2.0	1.37	0.81	1.62	0.58
3.0	1.18	0.70	1.22	0.44
5.0	0.95	0.56	0.90	0.32
7.0	0.79	0.47	0.77	0.28
10.0	0.63	0.38	0.66	0.24
13.0	0.51	0.31	0.61	0.22

[a]Price, in thousands of dollars for a ten thousand square foot lot, calculated using one of the following equations:

$$P_L = 1.70 - 0.46 * \text{Ln Distance} - .01 \text{ SIZLOT}$$
$$P_L = 0.44 + 2.37 * 1/\text{Distance} - .01 \text{ SIZLOT}.$$

estimates the price of land. Land prices seem low, especially within a radius of three miles of the CBD, which is largely within New Haven. The magnitude of the land prices can be explained in large measure by noting that these are prices for raw land only, excluding the values of locational amenities and all public services. An additional explanation might be that the logarithmic function is too inflexible to permit the prices of land close-in to be high and of land further out to be much lower.

To investigate this latter possibility, I have tried a second function to replace $f(D)$ in (5-4), the inverse function of distance. As compared to the logarithmic function, this implies a much more rapid initial decrease in land prices as the distance from the CBD increases. The coefficients for (5-4) when INVDST replaces LDST*A are found in Table 5-5, Column 2. Again, the individual coefficients are highly significant, though at somewhat lower levels than previously. Estimated land values at various distances are found in Columns 3 and 4 of Table 5-6. As expected, the implied land values within three miles of the CBD are substantially higher when INVDST is used rather than LDST*A, but for distances greater than this, the two functions yield virtually identical values. Because relatively few houses in this sample are located closer to the CBD than about 1.5 miles, not much weight can be attached to the rather different estimates of land prices close to the CBD. The great similarity between the land prices estimated by LDST*A and INVDST suggests that the apparently low value of land is not a consequence of the particular functional form used, but may be a reasonably correct estimate of the value of land without locational amenities or municipal services.

A third examination of the effect of accessibility on the rent gradient involved the gravity model, modified to recognize only two centers of economic activity: the CBD and the industrialized portion of tract 38. Using GRAVTY as the measure of accessibility, the coefficients have been estimated in Table 5-5, Column 3. According to equation (5-4), regression (3) contains a specification error, since the correct variable would be LOTSIZ*GRAVTY. Even so, the complete insignificance of the variable is somewhat surprising. In Column 4, the measure has been modified by using its natural logarithm, and in Column 5, elimination of the specification error substantially increases the significance of the coefficient for this measure of accessibility. Nevertheless, either of the simpler measures, LDST*A or INVDST, seems preferable.

In Table 5-7, the effect on land prices of allowing for the two centers of employment is shown by calculating the decline in land values as the distance from the CBD increases in various directions. Upon comparison of Tables 5-6 and 5-7, it is apparent that this more complicated procedure has changed the estimated land values very little, and that for the worse. Land values near New Haven CBD are estimated to be lower than before, and it would appear that the less rapid decline in prices to the north and north-east than in other directions does not agree as well with the observations as does the simpler assumption of a uniform decline.

Table 5-7. Estimated Land Values along Different Radii from the CBD

Sector	Miles from CBD	Miles from Second Job Center	GRAVTY	Land Value
Southwest	2	10.2	10.97	1.22
	5	12.4	4.51	0.88
	10	16.9	2.32	0.63
Northwest	2	7.8	11.06	1.22
	5	7.8	4.70	0.90
	10	10.0	2.44	0.65
North	2	6.6	11.13	1.23
	5	3.9	5.05	0.93
	10	2.5	3.36	0.77
Northeast	2	6.6	11.13	1.23
	5	3.8	5.07	0.93
	10	2.2	3.53	0.79
Southeast	2	7.8	11.06	1.22
	5	7.5	4.68	0.90
	10	9.4	2.46	0.65

Note: Land value, in thousands of dollars for a ten thousand square foot lot, calculated using the coefficients from Table 5-5, Column 5. The equation is

$$P_L = 0.32 - 0.01 * \text{SIZLOT} + 0.38 * Ln\,(\text{GRAVTY*SIZLOT}).$$

I have tried one more measure of accessibility: the time of travel from the CBD to the house, as obtained from the Skimtree matrix described in Chapter Two (Travel Times from the CBD). Since the travel time naturally incorporates the effects of increasing speeds with distance, there has been no attempt to make any nonlinear transformation of the variable, instead travel time in minutes simply replaces $f(D)$ in (5-4). The result is in Column 6 of Table 5-5. Increasing travel time is seen to exert a significant negative influence on land values, but to be a somewhat less valuable explanatory variable than either LDST*A or INVDST.

Before concluding this section, it is necessary to provide some evidence for a conclusion previously stated. In Chapter Two (Land Rent Gradient), the appropriateness of assuming equal transportation speeds in all directions from the CBD was discussed and provisionally accepted on the basis of evidence from the Skimtree matrix of travel time between tracts. In some directions, interstate highways passing near the CBD appeared to reduce by a substantial proportion the travel time required to go a fixed distance. Nevertheless, these cases were so few that it seemed no serious error would result if they were ignored in favor of the simpler assumption of equal speeds of travel.

At this point, I wish to examine my results for signs of error from this assumption. To do this, I have calculated the residuals from regression (1) of Tables 5-4 and 5-5, and have grouped them by tracts in Table 5-8. If the

Table 5-8. Residuals Grouped by Census Tract.

Tract	Average Residual[a]	Tract	Average Residual[a]
4	−1.2	36	1.2
5	−0.6	37	−0.6
6	−2.4	38	−1.8
7	−0.6	39	2.4
8	3.0	40	1.8
9	0.6	41.01 ⎫	
10	2.4	41.02 ⎭	−1.2
11	1.2	42	−0.6
12	0.6	43	−2.4
13	0.0	44	0.6
14	0.6	45	1.8
15	−1.2	46	−0.6
16	−3.0	47	2.4
18	1.2	48	0.0
19	1.2	49.01 ⎫	
20	−0.6	49.02 ⎭	1.2
24	3.6	50.01 ⎫	
25	−1.2	50.02 ⎪	
26	0.0	50.03 ⎬	1.2
27	−1.2	50.04 ⎭	
28	0.0	51	−1.2
29	−1.2	52	0.6
30.01 ⎫		54	0.0
30.02 ⎭	0.6	55	0.6
31.01 ⎫		56	1.2
31.02 ⎭	−0.6	57	0.0
32.01 ⎫		58	−1.2
32.02 ⎭	−1.8	59	0.0
33	−1.2	60	−1.2
34.01 ⎫		61	−1.8
34.02 ⎭	0.0	80[b]	−0.6
35.01 ⎫		90[c]	−1.2
35.02 ⎭	−1.2		

[a]Approximate median value of all observations in the tract.
[b]Tract 80 contains all of Cheshire.
[c]Tract 90 contains all of Wallingford.

Source: Residuals are the result of subtracting predicted prices from actual prices, using the coefficients of Tables 5-4 and 5-5, Column 1.

assumption of equal travel times in all directions is seriously wrong (and the equation is otherwise well-specified), then the residuals should have a perceptible pattern: for those tracts which are quickly reached, accessibility will be understated by the distance traveled. Consequently, land values should decline less than predicted, and residuals, on the average, should be positive. Similarly, the accessibility of tracts served by congested roads will be overstated by distance, and residuals, on the average, should be negative.

The hypothesis that positive residuals for observations in each tract

Table 5-9. Relation of Sign of Average Residual by Tract to Traffic Speed[a]

	Miles Per Hour			
	0-15	*15-20*	*20-24*	*25-*
Positive Residual	6 (5.59)[b]	10 (8.17)	3 (3.01)	2 (4.30)
Negative Residual	7 (7.43)	9 (10.86)	4 (4.00)	8 (4.57)
	$\chi^2 = 4.70$	d.f. = 3	$\chi^2_{0.05} = 7.82$	

[a]Tracts which had a zero average residual have been omitted.
[b]Expected values are in parentheses.

are independent of the rate of speed for travel to that tract can be tested in the 2 × 4 contingency table, Table 5-9, where the speeds from Table 2-2 are used to place the average residual from each tract into one of four speed classifications.[10] The Chi-square value is not significant at the 0.05 level, so the hypothesis of independence cannot be rejected at this level. Although the assumption undoubtedly introduces some error into the analysis, it seems that this is probably not a serious problem.

The Prices of Location Characteristics

To determine what part of the sales price of the combined housing bundle is spent for various locational advantages, the regressions include variables representing the provision of several public services, the presence of neighborhood amenities, and the magnitude of the property tax burden.

The discussion of the estimated coefficients, or hedonic prices, for these variables is concerned primarily with three issues: first, are subjective measures of neighborhood quality useful in explaining the different compositions and sales prices of housing bundles? Second, does it appear that property tax differentials are capitalized into the sales price of the housing bundle? Third, how successful are the objective measures of neighborhood characteristics in explaining variations in housing transaction prices? Do the objective and subjective measures play separate roles in setting prices; if so, how should they be used in a single regression?

Before these lengthy issues are taken up, however, it is convenient to examine the values placed on simple, specific municipal services. Dummy variables CWATER, CSEWER, GARBGE indicate the provision of city water, city sewage, and garbage collection to city residents free of explicit charges; that is, other than undifferentiated property taxes. Several important characteristics of these services should be noted. First, with the exception of New Haven it is not true

10. The tract average residual is, in this case, approximately the median value taken from a plot of residuals against tracts.

that if some houses in a town receive a service, all will;[11] consequently, the dummy variables will not act simply as town dummies. Second, it is not generally true that if a house has city sewerage it will also have city water. For towns other than New Haven the average correlation is about +0.3. This is of obvious importance for efforts to distinguish separate values for the two. Third, as noted in Chapter Four, there is little correspondence between a town's tax burden and the quality and scope of public services. Once again this is important for efforts to distinguish between tax and benefit capitalization.

Turning now to Table 5-5, it can be seen that the coefficients for CSEWER and GARBGE consistently have the anticipated positive signs and are usually statistically significant at at least the ten percent level (one-tail). The value attributed to the availability of city sewerage is reasonable, if perhaps a bit low; that for GARBGE is as appropriate as could be hoped. Private trash hauling is available in this area for a monthly fee of about $3.50, or $42.00 annually. In equations (1) and (2) the estimated coefficients for GARBGE are approximately $400, implying an annual capitalization rate of about 9%.[12] The negative sign for CWATER is contrary to my expectations, but some persons have suggested— only partly facetiously—that it is quite a reasonable reaction to the prospect of having to drink the heavily chlorinated municipal water. A more probable explanation is that the absence of CWATER is correlated with various locational amenities, since the houses lacking connections are generally those in isolated subdivisions within each town.

Subjective Evaluations. From Table 5-5, Column 1, it is apparent that subjective evaluations of neighborhood quality are useful in explaining the variation in the sales prices of housing bundles. Both GEN Q and SERVCE have the anticipated negative signs,[13] and both are significant at greater than the one per cent level. Furthermore, the variations in the prices of housing bundles in response to the neighborhood effects are not trivial: the coefficient for GEN Q implies that housing bundles with identical structural characteristics and equal accessibility to the CBD will sell in the worst neighborhood for $5,288 less than in the best; the difference in urban service levels will similarly result in a maximum price difference from this source of $2,228.[14] Inspection of Columns 2-6

11. Even in New Haven, a small fraction of homes received no city sewerage or water on account, apparently, of the place and date of construction.
12. The coefficient for GARBGE is somewhat sensitive to the treatment of CBD distance. The inner towns are more likely to offer collection, thus failure to capture the decline in land values as accessibility declines biases the coefficient on GARBGE upward, as in equations (3) and (4). When PRCNTL replaces GEN Q in (8) and (9), GARBGE becomes insignificant, which is not altogether surprising since PRCNTL was hypothesized to be a measure of fairly general public service characteristics.
13. Recall that a high score indicates an undesirable neighborhood.
14. The range of scores for GEN Q is −1.20 to 2.66; for SERVCE it is −1.66 to 4.53.

of Table 5-5 indicates that these estimates are largely unaffected by the various measures of accessibility examined.

Property Tax Capitalization. The discussion of tax capitalization in Chapter Four concluded that capitalization of tax differentials within a metropolitan area should be anticipated. Testing this is difficult, however, because of the problem of measuring the differential. Ideally, what one would wish to do is compare the actual tax to the tax liability were the same house located in the low-tax town; this is complicated by the fact that even within the low-tax town identical houses will generally have different assessments and different tax liabilities. Thus, a differential subject to capitalization exists in the low-tax town relative to the legal tax burden there, and in the other towns relative to the unknown legal burden in the low-tax town.

What is required is seemingly a way to predict the legal assessed value of houses in the low-tax town. If the assessment process were uniform so that identical houses paid identical taxes, this would be simple. The known market value in the low-tax town would not incorporate any effects of tax differentials; therefore, the legal assessed value would be the statutory percentage of market value, and an equation to predict this as a function of housing characteristics could be developed readily. Unfortunately, that is not so: assessments are not uniform; differentials exist; and market values should reflect these.

Despite these problems, the best approach still appeared to be the estimation of an equation predicting assessed value in North Haven (the low-tax town) as a function of housing characteristics. Provided the assessment methods are not too erratic, this should yield a reasonably good tool for predicting assessed values. The equation for assessed value proved, however, to be unsatisfactory, having a relatively large standard error and signs on individual coefficients contrary to expectations. Inasmuch as the assessment methods are known to produce quixotic variations, this outcome should not be surprising. Using the equation to predict differentials, one obtains for each observation:

Tax Differential = Actual mill rate · actual assessed value—low-tax mill rate
· predicted assessed value.

Regressions incorporating these differentials indicated them to be strongly significant, but positively related to sales price. This result is contrary to any reasonable hypothesis of capitalization; and in view of the unsatisfactory equation estimating assessed value, the method was dropped.[15]

Given the difficulty of calculating the differential, is there some way to avoid using it? One possibility might be to substitute total tax burden for the

15. It should be noted that the coefficients for GEN Q and SERVCE were virtually unchanged in all the experiments with alternative measures of tax burdens.

differential and examine for capitalization. This was done, but with unacceptable results. Total taxes were positively and significantly related to sales price, indicating that whatever the deficiencies of the assessment procedures, assessed values and therefore taxes usually rise and fall with market values. A second possibility, used in some previous studies, would measure the tax burden by the effective mill rate on property [30] [34]. This is unacceptable for several reasons, the most important being that a coefficient for the tax rate alone would imply a tax effect equal for all properties in each town. The market value of mansions would by implication be depressed just as much as that of modest homes. This treatment of the tax burden would therefore imply very slight capitalization for expensive dwellings and possibly more than full capitalization for cheap ones.

A third possibility, closer in spirit to the ideal and with some particular merit of its own, was actually adopted. Instead of trying to calculate what the assessed value of each home would be if it were in the low-tax town, it was assumed that buyers would compare the actual tax burden to the liability if the same assessed value were taxed at the low-tax mill rate. That is,

TAXDIF = Actual mill rate · assessed value—low-tax mill rate · assessed value.

This procedure assumes that buyers are aware of variations in the mill rate between towns but perceive no systematic variations in assessments between towns. The latter aspect is not so implausible as it may at first seem. We have already seen that assessments are capricious in detail (though generally rising and falling with market value), one indication being the wide range of assessment/ market value ratios shown in Table 4-8. This would make it difficult for buyers to predict with any confidence that assessed value in another town would be systematically different from that observed. Furthermore, despite wide variations in statutory assessment/market value ratios by town, Table 4-7 shows the average ratio in each town to be close to 0.5. On average, then, buyers would be reasonably correct in judging the assessed value of a dwelling to be about the same in the low-tax town as where it is.

Compared to the ideal measure first described, TAXDIF has the advantage of avoiding calculations perhaps unrealistically complex and offers considerable plausibility. It is important, then, to find that tax differentials so measured have quite modest effect on property values. The coefficient of TAXDIF in regression (1) of Table 5-5 is only -0.22 and is statistically insignificant. The negative sign is as anticipated by the hypothesis of tax capitalization, but the small size and insignificance of the variable provide little additional support.

Probably the most obvious explanation for the absence of tax capitalization is that already hinted at in Chapter Four: the assessed value of property for tax purposes is such an irregular proportion of market value that buyers may be unable to discern differentials which result from statutory tax rates or to separate them from differentials which reflect poor or obsolete assessments. The latter could disappear at any time and, consequently, would be expected to have little effect on market value. Since differentials resulting from assessment irregularities are as large and frequent in this sample as are those resulting from differences in the effective statutory tax rate, this explanation of the result in regression (1) may be quite important.

Though full capitalization of tax differentials is rather clearly excluded by the results of regression (1), an alternative explanation is possible which would admit some partial capitalization. New Haven and East Haven have the highest tax rates in the region, and they include some of the least desirable neighborhoods in the region, as measured by GEN Q. In contrast, neighborhoods in Orange and North Haven enjoy low taxes and favorable ratings on GEN Q. Similarly, East Haven has the highest equalized tax rate in two of the three years and by far the worse SERVCE of any town studied. Thus, it may be that multicollinearity between TAXDIF and the subjective evaluations of neighborhood amenity is responsible for the implied absence of tax capitalization.[16] What can be shown, however, is that even when very generous allowance for the existence of multicollinearity is made, full capitalization of property tax differentials is quite implausible.

The degree to which multicollinearity may be the cause of the apparent lack of tax capitalization can be indicated by making assumptions about which variable of a correlated pair is the "true" cause of the observed effect. That is, by attributing all the common variation of GEN Q and of TAXDIF to the latter, it is possible to establish an upper bound for the influence it has on PRICE.

To do this, I have used a technique suggested by Ridker and Henning [37] in a similar circumstance. Using GEN Q and SERVCE as dependent variables and TAXDIF as an independent variable, two auxiliary regressions are estimated. The residuals from these regressions are used as independent variables in regressions like (1) of Table 5-5, replacing whatever was the dependent variable of the auxiliary regression. Thus, instead of using GEN Q in regression (1), one uses RGEN Q—the vector of residuals from the regression of GEN Q on TAXDIF. These residuals will be orthogonal to TAXDIF and, therefore, will not bias the estimated coefficient for the variable in the later regression.

The effect of this procedure is to attribute to the variables used as independent variables in the auxiliary regressions all the covariation between them and the dependent variable. Thus, a subsequent regression which includes TAXDIF, RGEN Q, and RSERVCE will estimate the coefficient of TAXDIF to

---

16. The correlation between TAXDIF and GEN Q is +0.47 and that between TAXDIF and SERVCE is +0.28. Note that these correlations indicate a tendency for high-tax towns to have *less desirable* neighborhoods and offer *poorer* quality services.

Table 5-10. Auxiliary Regressions to Examine Effect of Multi-collinearity on Evidence of Tax Capitalization

Independent Variables	Dependent Variable			
	GEN Q		*SERVCE*	
Intercept	−0.567	(31.99)	−0.210	(7.43)
TAXDIF	3.45	(23.22)	3.00	(12.61)
	Summary Statistics			
S.E.E.	0.62		0.99	
R−square	0.22		0.08	
d.f.	1890		1890	
F−statistic	538.93		158.90	

Note: Figures in parentheses are *t*−values.

be what it would if GEN Q and SERVCE had simply been omitted. The joint explanatory power of the set of variables has been allocated to TAXDIF which makes this estimate of its influence an upper bound. The advantage of this procedure over simply omitting one or the other of a correlated pair of variables is that it allows one to retain all the explanatory power of both while assigning the joint variation to what is believed to be the true cause. The merit of this depends, quote obviously, on how strongly convinced one is of the true relationship.

Table 5-10 contains the estimated coefficients for the auxiliary regressions of GEN Q and SERVCE on TAXDIF. The new, residualized variables, RGEN Q and RSERVCE, are used in regression (7). As compared to its values in regressions (1) to (6), the coefficient of TAXDIF increases greatly in size and becomes highly significant, having a *t*-value of 5.63. The coefficient implies that each positive $100 tax differential will cause a decline in selling price of slightly more than $600. This result could be taken as support for the capitalization hypothesis; however, it should be emphasized that this value is an upper bound for the effect of tax differentials and is tenable only if one is willing to ascribe all the covariance of the subjective variables and the tax differentials to the latter. This is clearly a very strong assumption.

Some additional support for the capitalization hypothesis can be obtained from the results of regression (8) in which an objective measure of neighborhood quality—average percentile reading achievement score—replaces the subjective measure GEN Q. In this case, the coefficient for TAXDIF implies a smaller but statistically significant decrease in PRICE of $285 for each $100 positive tax differential. The coefficient for PRCNTL is large and highly significant, so that the apparent evidence of tax capitalization is not a result merely of the absence of any control for neighborhood quality. Nevertheless, if the earlier arguments for the desirability of including subjective measures of neighborhood amenity are correct, the coefficient for TAXDIF may gain much of its apparent size and significance from the bias caused by improperly excluding the subjective measure.

From regressions (1), (7), and (8), it is clear that neighborhood effects, including tax differentials, account for significant differences in the prices of housing bundles. What is uncertain is how, given the collinearity, this explanatory power should be allocated among TAXDIF, PRCNTL, GEN Q, and SERVCE. Since multicollinearity does not bias the point estimates of market prices in correctly specified equations, but only increases the estimated standard errors, the presumption must be that variations in perceived neighborhood quality have a more direct and significant effect on PRICE than do variations in property tax differentials. The relatively modest simple correlations of TAXDIF with GEN Q and SERVCE strengthen this general presumption.

Nevertheless, if full capitalization of tax differentials is rather clearly inconsistent with these results, it is possible to regard them as supporting partial capitalization. Such an interpretation would emphasize that TAXDIF consistently depresses market value, that correlations with GEN Q exist to reduce the "true" significance, and that with alternative measures of neighborhood quality TAXDIF has a sizeable and strongly significant effect. Moreover, the extent of capitalization, which may appear quite slight, is arguably more complete. Ordinarily, the degree of capitalization would be judged by comparing the reduction in market value to the present value of an infinite stream of fixed size. For example, a $1 tax differential persisting forever and discounted at 5% would be expected to reduce market value by $20. Thus, a $3 reduction would imply only about 15% of full capitalization. What this usual calculation overlooks, however, is the great uncertainty of future differentials which could reduce their expected value in the purchaser's eyes very rapidly to zero. For example, the $1 differential which the outside observer regards as persisting forever might actually be evaluated as equivalent to a series like $1, $1, $1, $1, $.9, $.6, $.5, $.4, $.3, $.2, $0.0, . . . The present value of this series, discounted at 5% is less than $6, rather than $20. The decline of $3 to $6 observed in regressions (8) and (9) would then represent 50% to 100% full capitalization as seen by the purchaser.

Subjective versus Objective Measures

The final issue to be examined in this section is the use of subjective rather than objective measures of neighborhood amenity to describe the housing bundle. In Chapter Four, it was argued that the subjective evaluations of each purchaser would be more appropriate and also better than objective measures: more appropriate because they describe precisely what the buyers *think* they have purchased; and better because of the great difficulties in creating satisfactory objective measures or in applying them once created. On the other hand, the rather high positive correlation was noted between neighborhood rankings on the basis of perceived and measured school quality. Thus, one might expect to find the advantage of the subjective measure less pronounced than the *a priori* arguments would suggest.

As explained previously, only two objective measures of neighborhood quality were available, both purporting to measure school quality. PRCNTL is the average score on a standard reading achievement test of pupils in the third or fourth grade of the neighborhood elementary school, and STRTIO is the overall pupil–teacher ratio for the school. Although it would be preferable to have many other measures, it is fortunate at least that an objective measure of school quality is probably as good a single objective index of neighborhood quality as one could devise. School quality may well be the most important characteristic of the neighborhood in view of prospective purchasers; moreover, a measure of school quality is likely to be highly correlated with other objective measures of neighborhood amenity.[17]

The two objective measures of neighborhood quality are used successively to replace GEN Q in regressions (8) and (9).[18,19] In regression (8), the coefficient of PRCNTL has the anticipated positive sign, is highly significant, and implies a variation of housing prices of about $3,000, since the range of average achievement scores by school is from almost zero to ninety-nine. In regression (9) GEN Q is replaced by STRTIO, but, as expected, the results are poor. The coefficient for STRTIO has the wrong sign and is insignificant, while that for TAXDIF rises absolutely with the implication that other variables have failed to control for the variations in neighborhood quality.

STRTIO is obviously not a good measure of neighborhood quality. On the other hand, PRCNTL appears to be quite successful: the *t*-value for the coefficient is very nearly as large as that for GEN Q and the *R*-square for the equation is about the same as that for an equation using GEN Q.[20] Thus, despite the *a priori* preference for a subjective measure, it must be admitted that either GEN Q or PRCNTL is about equally successful as an index of neighborhood amenity.

This conclusion is subject to some reservations, however. First, to some extent, the implication that regression (8) predicts PRICE about as well as does regression (1) is misleading. Because of the correlation between TAXDIF and GEN Q, the coefficient of TAXDIF is biased upward in absolute size and significance to compensate partially for the improper exclusion of the subjective measure. Thus, the influence of GEN Q is not altogether absent. Second, because

17. This was shown to be true of subjective measures in Table 5–3.

18. As a partial compensation for other, unavailable objective measures these regressions also include SERVCE. This subjective measure has a very low simple correlation with either objective measure; consequently, including it is unlikely to bias the estimated coefficient of either.

19. Because objective measures of school quality were unavailable for some schools, regressions (8), (9), (10), and (11) do not use the full sample of 1892 observations.

20. These comparisons refer to a regression like (1) but reestimated for the smaller sample.

of the correlation of +0.67 between GEN Q and PRCNTL, it is clear that for most neighborhoods either measure would do about equally well as a description of amenity levels. The choice between them should be made on the basis of their predictive value for the relatively few neighborhoods in which the difference between perceived and measured amenity is great; in these, the choice between GEN Q or PRCNTL will substantially change the estimated sum paid for amenity.[21] Although the advantage of the subjective measures is not universal, I conclude that in the cases for which a choice between measures would matter, the *a priori* arguments in favor of subjective measures remain convincing.

The preceding comments have been predicated on the need to choose between the objective and subjective measures; one might wish instead to use both. This is done in regression (10). Both GEN Q and PRCNTL remain highly significant; however, the existence of multicollinearity is evident from the decrease in the t-values for both. In addition, the R-square, adjusted for degrees of freedom, rises from 0.71 in regression (8) to only 0.72 in regression (20). Therefore, using both measures of neighborhood amenity in this way offers little advantage over using either one alone.

If it is supposed that objective and subjective measures can play different and distinctive roles, regression (10) is probably an incorrect way to investigate these roles. One could suggest that the subjective evaluation summarized in GEN Q necessarily builds upon and incorporates the "true" neighborhood differences which are measured by PRCNTL. These "true" variations are then modified and distorted by "halo effects," misinformation, and prejudice to yield the subjective ranking. Because it is an amalgam of objective and subjective differences, GEN Q is not an appropriate variable to use together with PRCNTL. What is necessary instead is a measure exclusively of the "halo effects," misinformation, and prejudice which cause GEN Q to deviate from the pure objective measure. One way to get this "purely" subjective index of amenity is to ascribe all of the covariance between PRCNTL and GEN Q to the former and create a new subjective measure which serves only to modify the objective measure.

This argument clearly invites the use of the residualization technique previously described. Regressing GEN Q on PRCNTL yields the following equation:

GEN Q = 1.28   - .021PRCNTL.
$\quad$ (26.30) $\quad$ (34.81) $\qquad$ $R^2 = 0.44$

The residuals from this regression have been used in regression (11) to replace GEN Q. With this change, the coefficient of PRCNTL increases substantially in size and significance, implying a maximum variation of housing bundle prices

21. This is true, for example, of the school district in New Haven, which was the best of all in terms of PRCNTL, but whose perceived quality was nevertheless quite low.

due to objectively measured neighborhood effects of about $4,000. "Residualized" GEN Q retains, of course, the coefficient and significance which it had in regression (10).

It should be emphasized that this procedure has not caused the estimated payment for amenity in any bundle to change. What it has done is to suggest that objectively measured differences among neighborhoods are somewhat more important in establishing location values than did regression (10). In addition, for those neighborhoods which enjoy approval out of proportion to their "true" merit, the effect of this perceived merit upon property values is also increased. For example, this procedure suggests that the good school districts in New Haven suffer from heavier misapprobation than is suggested by the score on GEN Q: for the scores on GEN Q to be no higher than they are, given the relatively good reading achievement test scores, the conviction must be especially strong that the schools are poor.

Is the procedure of residualizing GEN Q to obtain a "purely" subjective measure worthwhile? The answer must depend largely upon one's purposes in studying the housing bundle and one's views about the process which differentiates one neighborhood from another in terms of their amenity values. For predicting sales prices of housing bundles, it is apparent that either the objective PRCNTL or the subjective GEN Q will do about equally well. When both measures are available, but only one is to be used, GEN Q has considerable *a priori*, and a very slight statistical, advantage. But, if it is thought that neighborhoods are differentiated primarily on the basis of their "true" qualities rather than their perceived qualities, at least in the long run, then one would desire to emphasize the role of objectively measured differences. In this case, the residualization technique seems quite useful: it heavily weights the objective measure while preserving the important, though perhaps transitory, deviations due to perceived quality differences.

Chapter Six

The Evidence for Capitalization

The empirical work in the previous chapter provides answers to the questions which originally motivated this study. Households do perceive differences between neighborhoods in accessibility, public services, and amenities; and they are willing to pay more for residences in superior locations. All this is very much as one would expect. What was surprising, perhaps, was the evidence of, at most, partial tax capitalization despite quite substantial property tax differentials between adjacent towns. Making the most generous allowance possible, it was found that a $100 differential would depress sales prices by about $600. For comparison, a $100 differential expected to last forty years, and fully capitalized at 5 (8) % would reduce the sales price by $1,716 ($1,192). The evidence from this study is therefore that at most only 30% to 50% of full capitalization of tax differentials occurs. If one is willing to accept the argument that future differentials are highly uncertain, which would cause their expected value to go rapidly to zero, the apparent extent of capitalization would be greater. Nevertheless, it must be emphasized that to obtain statistically significant evidence of capitalization, it was necessary either to suppress the subjective measures of neighborhood quality or to make generous allowance for the influence of multicollinearity.

In general it is possible that differentials not capitalized into location values will be borne by immobile labor or that an initial decline in values will be tempered by an induced increase in demand for land. But for the area examined these possibilities are slight. Thus, the results imply that most or all of the tax differential is an excise tax on housing consumption. From this it follows that the apparent horizontal and vertical inequities of the tax system, described in Chapter Four, are largely real inequities.

The potential importance of these findings for policy decisions and studies of tax incidence makes it useful to be as precise about the implications as possible. It would be a mistake, I believe, to conclude from this study that full capitalization of taxes never or rarely occurs. A proper interpretation would seem to be that the extent of capitalization is critically dependent on the visibility and certainty of tax variations. When differentials arise mostly from assessment vagaries, capitalization is unlikely; but when tax changes occur which are more-or-less uniform and highly visible to potential buyers, full capitalization seems probable. A generalization—quite consistent with the implication of capitalization for assessibility, public services, and neighborhood amenities—might be: locational differences which are perceived and certain are capitalized; those which are not, are not. This may seem almost tautological, yet it serves to remind one that there is probably no single answer to the question: are taxes fully capitalized?

REVIEW OF PREVIOUS EMPIRICAL WORK

At the present time there are relatively few studies whose data base and methods of analysis are good enough to promote trust of their conclusions. Unfortunately, it is not really possible to judge how well even these conform to the generalization just presented because the studies which seem most reliable are also those examining the effects of sudden, dramatic revision of the entire tax system. At most it can be said that in the absence of highly visible changes, the evidence of capitalization is ambiguous.

Jensen

One of the earliest systematic investigations of property tax capitalization is contained in Jensen's classic volume, *Property Taxation in the United States,* [16], published in 1931. Here Jensen drew upon data collected by the U.S. Department of Agriculture for farms in fifteen counties throughout the United States. These data describe taxes, net rent per acre, and the value per acre in the years 1919 and 1924. Jensen observed that taxes rose substantially between the two years, from about 85 cents per acre to $1.38; net rents generally fell, and the percentage of rent taken in taxes rose from 22 to 31. Nevertheless, net rents relative to value per acre remained constant, averaging 2.3 percent in both years. This suggests capitalization: "the capital value is the elastic element, being depressed by rising taxes and falling rents, so as to leave the net rent, clear of taxes, at 2.3% for both years" [16, p. 73]. The analysis and data are both crude, and Jensen properly remarked that "there are too many as yet uncertain factors in the two basic variables, net returns and taxes, for anyone to be justified in pressing the conclusions very far" [16, p. 69]. Nevertheless, Jensen's results remained the best known study of capitalization for some thirty years.[1]

---

1. It is possible to apply more modern statistical methods to the data Jensen used. Daicoff [12, p. 57-8], for example, has used OLS regression to estimate the following equation:

Daicoff

A period of renewed interest in property tax capitalization began with Daicoff [12] in 1961. Daicoff analyzed three specially collected data sets, all far from ideal; but the analysis in each case rejected the hypothesis of capitalization. Using a set of aggregate data for twenty townships and three cities in Washtenaw County, Michigan, Daicoff found, for example:

$$\frac{\Delta V}{V_o} = 0.0782 + 14.96 \frac{\Delta T}{V_o} \qquad R = 0.53 \qquad \text{Standard error in parentheses}$$
$$\qquad\qquad\quad (4.77)$$

where

ΔV = change in aggregate value of rent property 1951-57
V_o = aggregate value of real property in 1951
ΔT = change in property tax collections 1951-57

$$\Delta V = 16.58 - 0.531\ V_o + 53.25\ \Delta T \qquad R = 0.86 \qquad \text{standard error in parentheses}$$
$$\qquad\quad (0.113) \qquad (9.55)$$

where

ΔV = change in value per acre from 1919 to 1924

V_o = value per acre in 1919

ΔT = change in tax per acre from 1919 to 1924

Since ΔT has a strongly significant positive coefficient, he concluded that the data do not support capitalization.

Daicoff's equation seems suspect because he has made no allowance for the considerable rise in general prices over the period 1919-24. In the equation estimated the only way this can be represented is through the coefficient for ΔT, and this might account for the positive sign. Using Jensen's data, I have tried alternative specifications, for example:

$$\text{VALU19} = 79.69 + 16.48\ \text{RENT19} + 8.82\ \text{TAX19} \qquad R = .77$$
$$\qquad\qquad\quad (6.17) \qquad\qquad (28.95)$$

or

$$\Delta\text{VALUE} = 67.60 + 38.82\ \Delta\text{TAXES} + 2.65\ \Delta\text{RENT} \qquad R = 0.67$$
$$\qquad\qquad\quad (19.22) \qquad\qquad (7.23) \qquad\qquad\qquad \text{standard error in parentheses}$$

where

VALU19 = value per acre in 1919
RENT19 = rent per acre in 1919
TAX19 = tax per acre in 1919
ΔVALUE = change in value per acre 1919-24
ΔTAXES = change in taxes per acre 1919-24
ΔRENT = change in rent per acre 1919-24

In neither case do land values per acre appear to be depressed by taxes; however, the positive coefficients have greatly reduced significance compared to Daicoff's equation. The differing results are possibly best regarded as indicating how uncertain is the implication of tax capitalization in these data.

Analysis of individual properties in Ann Arbor over the same period yielded the same conclusions. Daicoff regarded his work as strong evidence against capitalization:

> For the American real property tax, where most requirements for tax capitalization are met, all of the tests of the usually accepted doctrine produced results which are inconsistent with the doctrine. [12, p. 112]

As pieces of econometric work, Daicoff's analyses are unsatisfactory in many ways. As in the analysis of Jensen's data, the equations compare changes in values to changes in tax collections with no allowance for general price changes. For this reason alone, the coefficient on ΔT is likely to be positive. In addition, Daicoff's data lacked any description of public services, making it always possible that tax increases were accompanied by improved public services whose worth more than offset tax capitalization.[2] If so, the positive coefficient on taxes is not evidence against capitalization. For these and similar reasons, the conclusions properly drawn from Daicoff's study are more ambiguous than he recognized.

Wicks, Little, and Beck

More recently, Wicks, Little and Beck [47] have presented a study of capitalization of taxes on residential property in Montana. The circumstance inviting analysis was a general reassessment of property coupled with changes in the tax mill rate. Because of reassessment the relative tax burdens in the subsequent period were substantially altered. Wicks *et. al.* observed that if capitalization occurred, a change in the market value of any home between the periods before and after the reassessment should be related to the changed tax burdens. Analyzing sixty-four residential sales, they found that homes with large tax increases did, in fact, sell for less than would otherwise have been expected. On average, a $1 tax increase seemed to reduce market value by $19, suggesting a rate of capitalization of about 5%.

Smith

The Wicks, Little, and Beck study suffered from a small data base and crude analysis. A very similar, but much improved study is that of Smith for the city of San Francisco [43]. Once again, what made the study possible was a sudden, widely announced change in assessments. Prior to 1967 the various classes of residential and commercial property were assessed at very different proportions of market value, in the fashion described for Boston in Chapter Four.

---

2. For Ann Arbor some crude examination of this possibility yielded contrary evidence. Over the period examined, virtually the only change in public services was the construction of new schools in some areas. The average rates of appreciation of homes in areas with new schools was, however, only very slightly and insignificantly greater than the rate elsewhere.

Single family residences were assessed at about 10%, two to four unit dwellings at 14%, five or more unit dwellings at 20%, and commercial property at 20 to 25% of market value. Following approval of the Petrix-Knob Bill, uniform assessment ratios were required for all classes of property beginning in 1967; the obvious consequence was a dramatic increase in property taxes for many single-family homes.

For a sample of dwellings chosen from a relatively homogeneous part of the city, a method was developed for predicting sales price as a function of assessed value. As for Wicks, *et. al.* the method of analysis was to compare predicted sales price to actual sales price and relate any difference to a change in taxes. The comparisons, made in a number of ways, quite strongly support tax capitalization.

The weakness of this analytical method is the prediction of future sales prices in the absence of a tax change. If the equation developed should overestimate or underestimate prices, the effect of tax capitalization will seem either too large or too small. Since one test produced the implausible result of a $35 reduction in sales price for each $1 tax increase, this problem may be quite real. Nevertheless, other tests yielded more reasonable estimates and all indicated a reduction in sales price in response to a tax increase.

Orr

In a study of rental housing in the Boston metropolitan area, Orr [33] concluded that property tax differentials between jurisdictions were not shifted forward to occupants but were borne by the landlords. While this provides no direct evidence of capitalization, a presumption is established because the present value of net returns to buildings in high tax areas should otherwise be below the returns in low tax areas.

Orr's approach was similar to that of the present study, but the data available were much less satisfactory. Units of observation were entire towns and cities with only a few explanatory variables, such as the average price of land per acre, tax rate, educational expenditures, accessibility, and dummy variables for certain public services. Finding the tax rate to be an insignificant factor in explaining the median rent per room, Orr concluded that tax differentials are not shifted forward.

For a number of reasons Orr's work has been heavily criticized [14]. Though he studied rental property, the effective tax rate used was for single-family dwellings; as has been noted, different classes of property actually face quite different effective tax rates.[3] The denominator of his dependent variable, rent-per-room, was the median number of rooms in all units not just rental units. Other variables and units of observation were also considered inappropriate.

---

3. In fact, as Orr later admitted [34], the tax variable used was by mistake for all property, not single-family dwellings as originally stated.

After making the changes they deemed necessary, his critics obtained results which they considered nonsensical.

In a reply, Orr [34] demonstrated that specific aspects of the criticism are overly harsh. What emerges most clearly, however, is the sensitivity of the results to the precise variables used to explain rent levels. This is not particularly surprising, for Orr has used so few variables—and by implication omitted so many relevant ones—that the variables included will represent the influence of a multitude of improperly omitted, correlated variables. In this circumstance, it is difficult to know how any coefficients should be interpreted.

Oates

Probably the best known recent study of property tax capitalization is Oates' "test" of the Tiebout Hypothesis [30]. Tiebout [45] had argued that households would choose a residential community on the basis of its package of services and taxes. This implies that households will compete for desirable locations and will bid location rents up, capitalizing locational advantages. The empirical analysis is very similar to Orr's, except that Oates tries to explain the median value of single family homes in communities near New York City as a function of certain physical and locational characteristics. Because the tax rate in the equation has a negative strongly significant coefficient, Oates concludes that capitalization of the tax is observed;[4] more precisely, he suggests that about two-thirds of full capitalization occurs.

Oates' work is thoughtfully done; yet the data base seems inadequate for the use made of it, and there must consequently be some doubt about the reliability of the evidence. Oates, himself, recognized explicitly "the imprecision of several of the operational measures of the variables." Any difficulties from this are compounded in the analysis because Oates like Orr, used so few variables to explain variations of housing values that probable correlations with omitted variables will introduce biases difficult to anticipate. In this respect the use of the tax rate to describe the tax burden in various towns is particularly open to

4. The results of a TSLS estimation are:

$$V = -29 - 3.61nT + 4.91nE - 1.31nM + 1.6R + 0.06N + 1.5Y + .7P$$
$$\quad\ (2.3)(3.1) \quad\ (2.1) \quad\ \ (4.0) \quad\ \ (3.6) \quad (3.9) \quad (7.7) \ \ (3.1)$$

$R^2 = .93$ t values in parentheses

where

V = median value of single family homes in the community
T = Natural log of the effective percentage tax rate
E = Natural log of annual current expenditures per pupil in $ (1960–61)
M = Natural log of the linear distance in miles of the community from Mid–town Manhattan
R = Median number of rooms per owner–occupied house (1960)
N = Percent of houses built since 1950 (1960)
Y = Median family income in thousands of $ (1959)
P = Percent of families in the community with an annual income of less than $3,000 (1959).

question. As noted in Chapter Five this use carries the peculiar implication that the market value for all homes in the sample are depressed equally for equal tax rates. In effect the equation will suggest over-capitalization for low-priced homes and under-capitalization for expensive homes. Since this is improbable, it is quite likely that the tax coefficient is representing, in addition to any tax effect, systematic differences between cheap and expensive homes which were not explicitly included.

Moody

By far the most satisfactory examination of tax capitalization following a change in property taxes is Moody's recent study of San Francisco [26]. The basis for this is an unusual and extremely fine natural experiment. In 1962 voters in the San Francisco Bay area were asked to approve participation in the proposed Bay Area Rapid Transit System (BART). The cost of approval was the imposition of a special property tax throughout participating counties. In the closely contested poll, San Francisco chose to join but neighboring San Mateo County did not. Despite this outcome, earlier plans for placing a station precisely on the boundary between San Francisco and Daly City (in San Mateo) were retained. Thus, on one side of the border residents enjoy easy access to a modern rapid transit system without cost, on the other side residents have the access but must pay a property tax for the privilege.

Looking only at the San Francisco side of the boundary it would be difficult or impossible to separate any decrease in value following tax capitalization from an increase in value following accessibility benefit capitalization. But with the Daly City properties for comparison, this is possible. The essence of the analysis is shown in the simple diagram below. Prior to the transit system, housing prices are $OX. With the transit system suddenly added, there is a jump in house values on both sides of the boundary, assuming the benefits to be greater than the cost in San Francisco. $CA will be the capitalized benefit

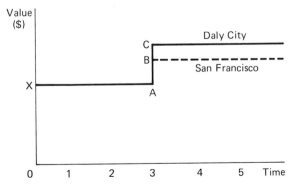

Figure 6-1. Capitalization of Transit Costs and Benefits

enjoyed by both areas, but the increment in land value observed in San Francisco is only $BA; the difference, $CB, will be the capitalized value of the additional property tax.

Analyzing sales records for some 1300 virtually identical single-family homes on both sides of the boundary, Moody found prices on the San Francisco side to be about $900 lower than in Daly City. The size of the reduction is rather large relative to the additional annual tax of $10-$15, but it is highly significant statistically and is certainly consistent with tax capitalization.

SUMMARY AND CONCLUSIONS

Whether or under what circumstances taxes are capitalized into location values remain somewhat unsettled issues. The studies by Smith and Moody imply relatively complete capitalization when tax changes are sudden and clearly visible. Oates' work implies substantial, though incomplete, capitalization of taxes even in normal circumstances, but the problems of interpreting his tax variable and making certain that the tax rate is not acting as a proxy for the many omitted variables suggest caution. Daicoff found no evidence of capitalization, but the results may possibly be explained by the lack of controls for public service variations and other econometric problems.

Examining the legal and illegal tax variations in the New Haven metropolitan region, this study found evidence of, at most, only limited tax capitalization. For a number of reasons these results seem particularly well founded. An empirical study is always limited not only *to* but also *by* the particular data set available. Fortunately, the data base analyzed here is uniquely suited to the demands made upon it, being large, detailed, and disaggregated. Since only houses just sold are examined, the sample is an equilibrium one, which is important to cross-sectional studies.

For the most part, the analysis was quite successful in *a priori* terms, isolating reasonable prices for a number of structural characteristics, perceived amenities, public services, and accessibility. The area studied seems favorable to tax capitalization because of its small size, good transportation system, and substantial tax variations between jurisdictions. Yet despite the favorable circumstances and appropriate data base there is no evidence of full capitalization. It is difficult, then, to avoid the conclusion that tax differentials are often not perceived—or perceived as not lasting—and hence not fully capitalized, especially when the existing assessment procedures make differentials obviously erratic and unreliable.

Bibliography

1. Adelman, Irma and Griliches, Zvi. "On an Index of Quality Change," *Journal of the American Statistical Association,* LVI (September, 1961), 535–48.
2. Allen, R.G.D. *Mathematical Analysis for Economists.* New York: St. Martin's Press, Inc., 1938.
3. Alonso, William. *Location and Land Use.* Cambridge: Harvard University Press, 1964.
4. Anderson, Robert J. and Crocker, Thomas D. "Air Pollution and Residential Property Values," *Urban Studies,* VIII (October, 1971), 171–80.
5. Bailey, M.J., Muth, R.F., and Nourse, H.O. "A Regression Method for Real Estate Price Index Construction," *Journal of the American Statistical Association,* LVIII (December, 1963), 933–42.
6. Becker, Gary S. "A Theory of the Allocation of Time," *The Economic Journal,* LXXV (September, 1965), 493–517.
7. Black, David E. "The Nature and Extent of Effective Property Tax Rate Variations Within the City of Boston," *National Tax Journal,* XXV (June, 1972), 203–10.
8. Brigham, Eugene F. "The Determinants of Residential Land Values," *Land Economics,* XLI (November, 1965), 325–34.
9. Brown, H.G. *The Economics of Taxation.* New York: Holt, 1924.
10. Copes, John M. "Reckoning With Imperfections in the Land Market." *The Assessment of Land Value,* Edited by Daniel M. Holland. Madison, Wisc.: The University of Wisconsin Press, 1970.
11. Cramer, J.S. *Empirical Econometrics.* New York: American Elsevier Co., 1969.
12. Daicoff, Darwin W. "Capitalization of the Property Tax," Unpublished Ph.D. Dissertation, Department of Economics, University of Michigan, 1961.
13. Harris, R.N.S., Tolley, G.S, and Harrell, C. "The Residence Site Choice," *Review of Economics and Statistics,* L (May, 1968), 241–7.

14. Heinberg, J.D. and Oates, W.E. "The Incidence of Differential Property Taxes on Urban Housing: A Comment and Some Further Evidence," *National Tax Journal,* XXIII (March, 1970), 92–8.

15. Hirsch, Werner Z. "The Supply of Urban Public Services," *Issues in Urban Economics.* Edited by Harvey S. Perloff and Lowdon Wingo, Jr. Baltimore: The Johns Hopkins Press, 1968.

16. Jensen, Jens Peter. *Property Taxation in the United States.* Chicago: The University of Chicago Press, 1931.

17. Kain, John F. and Quigley, John M. "Measuring the Value of Housing Quality," *Journal of the American Statistical Association,* LXV (June, 1970), 532–48.

18. King, A. Thomas. "The Demand for Housing: A Lancastrian Approach," Mimeo, 1973.

19. Kmenta, Jan. *Elements of Econometrics.* New York: The Macmillan Co., 1971.

20. Labovitz, Sanford. "The Assignment of Numbers to Rank Order Categories," *American Sociological Review,* XXV (June, 1970), 515–24.

21. McDonagh, Edward C. and Rosenblum, Abraham L. "A Comparison of Mailed Questionnaires and Subsequent Structured Interviews," *Public Opinion Quarterly,* XXIX (Spring, 1965), 131–6.

22. Margolis, Julius. "The Demand for Urban Public Services." *Issues in Urban Economics.* Edited by Harvey S. Perloff and Lowdon Wingo, Jr., Baltimore: The Johns Hopkins Press, 1968.

23. Meyer, John R. "Urban Transportation." *The Metropolitan Enigma.* Edited by James Q. Wilson. Cambridge: Harvard University Press, 1968.

24. Mieszkowski, Peter. "The Property Tax: An Excise Tax or a Profits Tax?" *Journal of Public Economics,* I (April, 1972), 73–96.

25. Mills, Edwin S. *Studies in the Structure of the Urban Economy.* Baltimore: The Johns Hopkins Press for Resources for the Future, Inc., 1972.

26. Moody, James P. "Measuring Tax and Benefit Capitalization From a Local Rapid Transit Investment in the San Francisco Bay Area." Unpublished, preliminary results for Ph.D. Dissertation, University of California, Berkeley, (February, 1973).

27. Musgrave, John C. "The Measurement of Price Changes in Construction." *Journal of the American Statistical Association,* LXIV (September, 1969), 771–86.

28. Muth, Richard F. *Cities and Housing.* Chicago: University of Chicago Press, 1969.

29. Netzer, Dick. "Impact of the Property Tax: Its Economic Implications for Urban Problems," U.S. Congress, Joint Economic Committee and the National Commission on Urban Problems, Washington, D.C.: U.S. Government Printing Office, 1968.

30. Oates, Wallace E. "The Effects of Property Taxes and Local Public Spending on Property Values," *Journal of Political Economy,* LXXVII, (November/December, 1969), 957–71.

31. Oldman, Oliver and Aaron, Henry. "Assessment–Sales Ratio Under the Boston Property Tax," *National Tax Journal,* XVIII (March, 1965), 36–49.

32. Oppenheim, A.N. *Questionnaire Design and Attitude Measurement.* New York: Basic Books, 1966.

33. Orr, Larry L. "The Incidence of Differential Property Taxes on Urban Housing," *National Tax Journal,* XXI (September, 1968), 172–80.

34. Orr, Larry L. "The Incidence of Differential Property Taxes on Urban Housing: A Response," *National Tax Journal,* XXIII (March, 1970), 99–101.

35. Pendleton, William C. "The Value of Highway Accessibility," Unpublished Ph.D. Dissertation, Department of Economics, University of Chicago, 1963.

36. Richman, R.C. "The Incidence of Urban Real Estate Taxes Under Conditions of Static and Dynamic Equilibrium," *Land Economics,* XLIII (May, 1967), 172–80.

37. Ridker, R., and Henning, J.A. "The Determinants of Residential Property Values with Special Reference to Air Pollution," *Review of Economics and Statistics,* XLIX (May, 1967), 246–57.

38. Rogers, Daniel C. "Private Rates of Return to Education in the United States: A Case Study," Unpublished Ph.D. Dissertation, Department of Economics, Yale University, 1967.

39. Rolph, E.R. and Break, G. *Public Finance.* New York: Ronald Press, 1961.

40. Scott, Christopher. "Research on Mail Surveys," *Journal of the Royal Statistical Society,* XXIV, Series A (1961), 143–95.

41. Sellitz, Clarie; Johoda, Marie; Deutsch, Morton; and Cook, Stuart W. *Research Methods in Social Relations.* New York: Holt, Rinehart, Winston, Inc., 1967.

42. Simon, H.A. "The Incidence of a Tax on Urban Real Property," *Quarterly Journal of Economics,* LVII (May, 1943), 398–420.

43. Smith, Stafford. "Property Tax Capitalization in San Francisco," *National Tax Journal,* XXIII (June, 1970), 177–94.

44. The Twentieth Century Fund. *American Housing: Problems and Prospects.* New York: The Twentieth Century Fund, 1944.

45. Tiebout, C. "A Pure Theory of Local Expenditures," *Journal of Political Economy,* LXIV (October, 1956), 416–24.

46. Weicher, John C. and Zerbst, Robert H. "The Externalities of Neighborhood Parks: An Empirical Investigation," *Land Economics,* XLIX (February, 1973), 99–105.

47. Wicks, John H.; Little, Robert A.; and Beck, Ralph A. "A Note on Capitalization of Property Tax Changes," *National Tax Journal,* XXI (September, 1968), 263–66.

48. Wieand, Kenneth F. "Air Pollution and Property Values: A Study of the St. Louis Area," *Journal of Regional Science,* XIII (April, 1973), 91–6.

49. Wihry, David. "Price Discrimination in Metropolitan Housing Markets," Unpublished manuscript, 1969.

50. Wingo, Lowdon, Jr. *Transportation and Urban Land.* Washington, D.C.: Resources for the Future, 1961.

Index

accessibility, 13; gravity model, 82; rent gradients, 2; theoretical models, 1; total sale price, 58
achievement scores, 57
air pollution, 64
amenities, 54; in a model, 10; payment, 94; sales price, 12; subjective evaluations, 86; value test, 57
Ann Arbor, 95
assessment: ratios, 47; ratio and blacks, 48; differentials, 87; tax rates, 52

BART (Bay Area Rapid Transit System), 97
Becker, G., 9
Black, D., 47
blacks: and assessment, 48
Boston, 47, 98
budget: constraints in a model, 84

capitalization: and tax differential, 91–95; tax and benefit, 86
CBD (central business district), 9; land values, 82; travel time, 18–21
commuting: and labor force, 51
crime rate, 56

Daicoff, D., 97–102
Daly City, 101
development, 50
differentials: intratown, 54
diversity, 43

East Haven, 62; and tax rates, 45
education, 55; as indicator in survey, 37; methodology in measurement, 46
excise tax, 49; tax differentials, 51

freeways, 17

Gates, Paul, 27
gravity: concept and accessibility measure, 14

halo effects, 65
Hamden, 64
hedonic prices, 5
Hirsch, W., 56
housing: analysis of transactions, 67; apartments, 47; definition, 68; bundle and characteristic evaluation; bundle and components, 23; bundle and tax burden, 52; bundle and tax differential, 83; definition, 5; single family units, 25; value, 49

income, 55; and house purchase, 35; survey response, 40; upper brackets, 49
inequitites: in taxes, 47

Jensen, J., 96

Kain, J. and Quigley, J., 56
Kmenta, J., 78

Labovitz, S., 61
land: as a commodity, 67; as a component, 8; prices, 70; prices and accessibility, 81; quantity and amenities, 73; rent gradient, 13; value variables, 72
location: amenity, 72; characteristics, 11, 60; characteristics as a commodity, 67; characteristics and price, 85; as a component, 8; rents, 51; value, 49; value and differentials, 95

McDonagh, E. and Rosenblum, A., 33
mail survey, 29; and Oppenheim, 36
Margolis, J., 56

About the Author

A. Thomas King graduated from Stanford University in 1966 with an A.B. Honors included the award of a National Science Foundation Fellowship for graduate study and membership in Phi Beta Kappa. Graduate training was at Yale University, where he received an M.Phil. (1969) and a Ph.D. (1972). His special interests are in urban and regional economics and public finance.

He is presently a Research Associate in the Bureau of Business and Economic Research at the University of Maryland and holds a joint appointment as Assistant Professor in the Department of Economics.

Research papers include "Racial Discrimination, Segregation, and the Price of Housing" (with Peter Mieszkowski) in the *Journal of Political Economy,* "The Demand for Housing: A Lancastrian Approach," and "State and Local Public Sector Accounts for Maryland" (with Ray D. Whitman). He is currently completing a study of housing demand.